LISTENING POWER 2

Language Focus • Comprehension Focus • Note-Taking Skills • Listening for Pleasure

David Bohlke

Bruce Rogers

PEARSON
Longman

Listening Power 2

Copyright © 2011 by Pearson Education, Inc.
All rights reserved.

Pearson Education, 10 Bank Street, White Plains, NY 10606

Staff credits: The people who made up the *Listening Power* team, representing editorial, production, design, manufacturing, and marketing are John Brezinsky, Dave Dickey, Nancy Flaggman, Ann France, Amy McCormick, Liza Pleva, Jaimie Scanlon, Loretta Steeves, and Paula Van Ells.

Text composition: TSI Graphics
Text font: 11.5/13 Caslon
Illustrations: TSI Graphics
Credits: See page 151.

Library of Congress Cataloging-in-Publication Data
Rogers, Bruce
    Listening power. 1 : language focus : comprehension focus : listening for pleasure / Bruce Rogers, Dorothy Zemach.
        p. cm.
    ISBN 0-13-611421-0 — ISBN 0-13-611425-3 — ISBN 0-13-611428-8
    1. English language—Textbooks for foreign speakers. 2. Listening. 3. Reading comprehension.
I. Zemach, Dorothy II. Title.
    PE1128.R63446 2011
    428.3'4—dc22

                                                                    2010043222

ISBN-10: 0-13-611425-3
ISBN-13: 978-0-13-611425-3

PEARSONLONGMAN ON THE **WEB**

Pearsonlongman.com offers online resources for teachers and students. Access our Companion Websites, our online catalog, and our local offices around the world.

Visit us at **pearsonlongman.com**.

Printed in the United States of America
1 2 3 4 5 6 7 8 9 10—V042—15 14 13 12 11 10

Contents

Acknowledgments

The authors of *Listening Power 2* would like to thank Amy McCormick for her guiding vision for the book and the series; Jaimie Scanlon for her skillful and thorough editing of the manuscript; Loretta Steeves for her work in shaping the project and bringing it to completion; our fellow Listening Power authors Tammy LeRoi Gilbert and Dorothy Zemach for their feedback, suggestions, and encouragement. We'd also like to thank the entire staff at Pearson Longman for a job well done.

The authors and publisher would also like to extend special thanks to the following teachers around the world who reviewed the *Listening Power* series and provided indispensable feedback.

Abigail Brown, Assistant Professor, TransPacific Hawaii College; Alison Evans, Senior Instructor, University of Oregon; Amy Christensen, Instructor, Central New Mexico Community College; Matthew Fryslie, Instructor, Kainan University; Ian K. Leighton, Instructor, SungKyun Language Institute; Rosa Vasquez, Instructor, John F. Kennedy Institute of Languages.

David Bohlke   Honolulu, Hawaii
Bruce Rogers   Boulder, Colorado

About the Authors

David Bohlke has over twenty years of experience as a teacher, teacher trainer, program director, editor, and materials developer. He has taught in universities, high schools, language institutes, and corporations in Japan, Korea, Saudi Arabia, and Morocco and has conducted multiple teacher-training workshops in the Middle East and Africa. He is currently based in Sydney, Australia.

Bruce Rogers has taught language and test preparation courses to English language learners since 1979. He taught at the Economics Institute, University of Colorado, Boulder for twenty-one years. He has also taught in Indonesia, Vietnam, Korea, and the Czech Republic. He is the author of six other textbooks for English language learners and is the past president of Colorado TESOL. He lives and works in Boulder, Colorado, USA.

Introduction to *Listening Power 2*

To the Teacher

Helping students develop strong listening skills is an important part of any language program. Good listening skills are a necessity in the classroom and the workplace, as well as in social interactions. In addition, standard English-language tests, such as TOEFL©, TOEIC©, and IELTS©, also require solid skills in listening. Listening was once considered a passive skill, but research has shown that successful listening requires the listener's active engagement. Listening is also considered by many learners to be the most challenging language skill.

The *Listening Power* series is designed to help learners meet the challenges of listening in English and provide students with the effective listening strategies that they need. It also provides a wealth of practice materials designed to facilitate listening fluency.

Listening Power 2 has four separate parts, each related to one of four important elements of effective listening. Unlike other listening skills programs, *Listening Power* does not require classes to begin with the first unit and work their way page by page to the end. Teachers and students are encouraged to skip from part to part and unit to unit.

Part 1: Language Focus—The units in this section target specific language skill areas that are often challenging for learners when they listen. These include understanding various types of questions, common reduced forms (such as "wanna" and "gonna"), homophones (such as "sweet" and "suite"), and sentence stress patterns. After each **Skill Presentation,** there is a set of practice activities, followed by the **Put It Together** section, which provides consolidated practice with longer, more challenging listenings centered on an interesting topic or theme. Teachers may choose to have students complete Put It Together exercises immediately after completing the skill sections or use them for later review.

Part 2: Comprehension Focus—This part of the text includes two sub-sections. The units in the **Building Skills** section present skills required to comprehend longer conversations and lectures, such as finding the main idea, understanding details, making inferences, and understanding the sequence of events in a talk. Each Building Skills unit includes integrated practice activities. The **Applying Skills** units offer high-interest, theme-based listening texts and additional practice activities designed to help students put their new skills to practical use.

Part 3: Note-Taking Skills—The ability to take clear and complete notes is one of the most important aspects of academic listening. This part of the text guides students through the basics of effective note taking: writing down only key words, using abbreviations and symbols, and separating important ideas from inessential or irrelevant details.

Part 4: Listening For Pleasure—This part of the book is just for fun! Lessons are designed to build students' confidence in listening by presenting enjoyable, motivating topics and contexts, such as TV shows and stories. These lessons can be used at any time during the course to provide a change of pace and to show students that listening can be interesting and pleasurable.

Although the unit structure varies somewhat from part to part, most of the longer listenings follow this pattern:

Unit Warm Up: These activities activate students' prior knowledge of the topic.

Before You Listen: This section includes a **Vocabulary Preview** which targets high-frequency, useful words from the listening text. In addition, students have an opportunity to predict the listening content.

While You Listen: Students listen and complete one or more tasks which practice what they learned in the Skill Presentation.

After You Listen: These activities integrate speaking to reinforce the target listening skills. Tasks are designed to stimulate discussion and critical thinking about issues raised in the listening.

A wide variety of topics are discussed in *Listening Power*. All were chosen to be engaging and of high interest to as many learners as possible.

The authors of the *Listening Power* series hope that both you and your students find this series useful and enjoyable.

To the Student

Welcome to Listening Power!

Listening is a very important language skill. Most people spend more time listening than they do speaking, reading, or writing. Listening is important in the classroom, at work, and in social situations. However, learning to listen in another language can be difficult. When you listen to a TV show, movie, lecture, or conversation in English, you may feel overwhelmed and "tune out" (stop listening).

Listening Power will help you improve your listening skills. You'll practice listening to conversations, mini-lectures, stories, and parts of TV shows. As you listen, you'll complete different types of practice activities to help you build useful vocabulary and understand and respond to what you hear in English.

You will have opportunities to work individually, in pairs or small groups, and as a whole class. To get the most out of this course, when you listen, you need to relax and focus on just listening; try not to think of other things. You also need to participate fully in the group activities and discussions. Don't worry if you don't understand everything that you hear or if you cannot complete a task. If you have problems, ask your teacher to repeat a listening or help you with an activity.

Listening Power 2 is divided into four parts. Each part focuses on one important element of listening, so it is like four books in one. However, you do not have to complete the parts in order. You and your teacher are encouraged to move from part to part and from unit to unit and work on the skills that you and your classmates need the most.

Part 1: Language Focus—The units in this part focus on language skill areas that are often challenging for learners at the intermediate level: understanding various types of questions, reduced forms (such as "I gotta" in place of "I've got to"), homophones (such as "sail" and "sale"), and sentence stress patterns. After each Skill Presentation, you will complete several practice activities. The **Put It Together** section at the end of the unit provides more practice with longer, more challenging listening materials.

Part 2: Comprehension Focus—This part has two sections. In **Building Skills,** you will listen to longer conversations and talks, and practice comprehension skills such as understanding main ideas and details, understanding the sequence of events in a talk, and drawing inferences. The **Applying Skills** units offer interesting listening texts and additional practice activities to help you use your new listening skills.

Part 3: Note-Taking—This part will help you learn the basics of effective note taking: writing down key words, using abbreviations and symbols, and separating important ideas from unimportant details.

Part 4: Listening For Pleasure—This part is just for fun! These lessons allow you to enjoy listening to things like an old-time radio show and stand-up comedy so that you can practice your listening skills while having fun at the same time.

To increase your skills, the authors recommend that you practice listening as much as possible and use your English whenever you can. Listen to radio shows and watch TV shows in English. Go to English-language movies. Take part in conversations in English. Visit websites that provide practice listening, such as those provided by the BBC© World Service, Voice of America: Learning English, radio shows on NPR®, and TED Talks.

We hope that you find this series useful and enjoyable.

David Bohlke
Bruce Rogers

PART
1

Language Focus

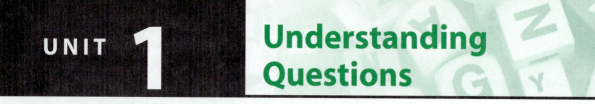

Understanding Questions

Unit Warm Up

A. *Match the questions to the answers.*

   e   1. Is our teacher Canadian?   a. He's Canadian.

_____ 2. Where is our teacher from?   b. Yes, I do. He's from Canada.

_____ 3. Is our teacher American or Canadian?   c. Canada.

_____ 4. Do you know where our teacher is from?   d. No, he's not. He's Canadian.

_____ 5. Our teacher isn't American, is he?   e. Yes, he is.

B. *Work with a partner. Think of three questions you'd like to ask your teacher. Then ask them.*

SKILL PRESENTATION

There are several different kinds of questions in English. Being aware of the different types of questions can help you know what kinds of information people are asking for and how to respond. Look at the questions in the Unit Warm Up. How are they different? How are the answers different? In this unit, you will practice listening and responding to different types of questions.

Yes/No Questions

We ask this type of question when the expected answer is either *yes* or *no*. *Yes/No* questions begin with auxiliary verbs and the verb *be*, for example *are, is, does, did, was, were, have, will, would, can,* and *should*.

A. 🎧 *Listen to the questions and responses.*

Questions	Responses
1. Are you from around here?	Yes, I am.
2. Did she grow up in Mexico City?	No, she didn't.
3. Can they sing and dance?	Yes, they can.
4. Is this bus going downtown?	Yes, it is.
5. Should we buy our tickets online?	No, you shouldn't.

B. 🎧 *Listen again and repeat the questions.*

Wh- Questions

We use *Wh-* questions to ask for specific information, such as a person's name, a price, where to meet someone, or the time an event starts or ends. *Wh-* questions begin with words such as *what, when, who, where, why, which, how, how many, how much, how long,* and *how often*.

A. 🎧 *Listen to the questions and responses.*

Questions	Responses
1. What's your name?	It's Carlos Sosa.
2. When was she born?	March 16, 1994.
3. How long have they lived here?	For about five years.
4. Why didn't you call me?	Sorry. I lost your number.
5. Who is your English professor?	Dr. Martin.

B. 🎧 *Listen again and repeat the questions.*

🎧 *Listen. Do you hear a* Yes/No *or a* Wh- *question? Write Y/N or Wh-.*

1. ____   2. ____   3. ____   4. ____   5. ____   6. ____

Alternative Questions

An alternative question includes two or more answer choices within the question itself. You can usually recognize an alternative question by listening for the word *or*.

Example
....

Do you prefer coffee or tea?

A. 🎧 **Listen to the questions and responses.**

Questions	Responses
1. Are you a junior or a senior?	I'm a junior.
2. Does he live on or off campus?	He lives on campus.
3. Did they sign up for the 10:00 or 2:00 class?	The 10:00 class.
4. Do you usually drive or take the bus to work?	I usually drive.
5. Is Charles English or Australian?	I think he's Australian.

B. 🎧 **Listen again and repeat the questions.**

Be careful! Some questions may look like alternative questions, but they are actually *Yes/No* questions.

Example
....

Do you have any brothers or sisters?

This question is asking about both brothers and sisters, not giving a choice.

Listening for the intonation of the question can tell you how to answer. The intonation in an alternative question rises and then falls. The intonation in *Yes/No* questions rises at the end.

C. 🎧 **Listen and repeat the questions.**

Alternative questions

Do you prefer coffee or tea?

Is your sister older or younger than you?

Yes/No **questions**

Does she have any dogs or cats?

Are there any letters or packages for me?

Would you like some coffee or dessert?

☑ **Check Yourself**

🎧 *Listen. Do you hear an alternative question? Write* Y *(yes) or* N *(no).*

1. _____   2. _____   3. _____   4. _____   5. _____   6. _____

Embedded Questions

An embedded question is included within another question.

Example

> *Do you know where the bank is?*

A. 🎧 *Listen to the questions and responses.*

Questions	Responses
1. Do you know what time it is?	Sure. It's 5:30.
2. Can you tell me who those people are?	Sorry. I don't know.
3. Do you have any idea if this class is full?	Yes, it's completely full.
4. Could you tell me when the next train is?	It's at 2:10.

B. 🎧 *Listen again and repeat the questions.*

> **Note**
>
> Using an embedded question can have a "softening" effect and often sounds more polite than a direct question.
>
> *Example*
>
> > *Where is the post office?* <u>vs.</u> *Can you tell me where the post office is?*
>
> Embedded questions look like *Yes/No* questions, but the expected answer is usually more than just yes or no. We generally answer *yes* or *no* and then add more information.
>
> *Example*
>
> > *A: Do you know when Tom's birthday is?*
> >
> > *B: Yes, I think it's September 3.*

🎧 *Listen. You will hear six embedded questions. Think about the answer for each one. Write the number of the question next to the correct answer.*

_____ **a.** Sorry. I'm not from around here.

_____ **b.** Yes. There was some bad weather.

_____ **c.** No. You will have to wait until class tomorrow.

_____ **d.** Yes. It's about two hours.

_____ **e.** Sure. It opens at 9:00 A.M. and closes at 5:00 P.M.

_____ **f.** I think it's around $300.

Tag Questions

Tag questions ask for confirmation or agreement. They consist of a statement and a tag.

Example

It's hot today, isn't it?
  statement   tag

In an affirmative sentence, the tag is negative. In a negative sentence, the tag is affirmative. Tags always use same verb tense as the statement.

🎧 *Listen and repeat the questions.*

Affirmative statement + negative tag	Negative statement + affirmative tag
1. It's a beautiful day, isn't it?	**1.** You didn't do your homework, did you?
2. Ann lives near here, doesn't she?	**2.** They haven't traveled overseas, have they?
3. You can read Arabic, can't you?	**3.** He shouldn't drive, should he?

Note
You can answer a tag question with *yes* or *no* and then give more information.

Example

A: You can speak Spanish, can't you?   *B: Yes, I can. I spent a year in Spain.*

B: Actually, no, but I can speak French and Italian.

A: You're not from around here, are you?   *B: Yes, actually, I am. I was born here.*

B: No. I moved here a few weeks ago.

☑ CheckYourself

A. 🎧 *Complete each statement with the correct tag. Then listen and check your answers.*

1. The weather is really nice today, _____?

2. You don't play the piano, _____?

3. Sometimes English spelling doesn't make sense, _____?

4. You're trying to improve your listening skills in English, _____?

5. All of your friends have cell phones, _____?

6. Your best friend can speak three languages, _____?

B. *Work with a partner. Ask and answer the questions above. Answer with your own information.*

PRACTICE

■ EXERCISE 1

Read these questions. Think about your answers. Then ask and answer the questions with a partner.

1. Are you single or married?

2. Where do you live?

3. Have you lived there long?

4. What do you like to do in your free time?

5. Do you take the bus to class?

6. Are you taking any other classes?

7. Do you know where our teacher is from?

8. How many brothers and sisters do you have?

9. What goals do you have for this class?

10. This class is fun so far, isn't it?

Example
....

A: Are you single or married?

B: I'm married. How about you? Are you single or married?

◼ EXERCISE 2

A. 🎧 *Listen. You will hear ten questions. Check (✓) the best answer.*

1. a ☐ Several times a day.   b ☐ I don't think so.

2. a ☐ Pizza.   b ☐ Yes, I am.

3. a ☐ Yes, it is.   b ☐ It's sunny and warm.

4. a ☐ It's easier.   b ☐ Math.

5. a ☐ Coffee shop.   b ☐ No, I don't.

6. a ☐ My mother, I think.   b ☐ They're my parents.

7. a ☐ Yes, he does.   b ☐ He's a teacher.

8. a ☐ No, I don't.   b ☐ Just one friend.

9. a ☐ No, I haven't.   b ☐ I just got a new TV.

10. a ☐ Probably about thirty.   b ☐ Yes, they do.

B. 🎧 *Listen to the questions again. Answer with your own information.*

1. _____.
2. _____.
3. _____.
4. _____.
5. _____.
6. _____.
7. _____.
8. _____.
9. _____.
10. _____.

◼ EXERCISE 3

🎧 *Listen to the two phone conversations. Answer the questions.*

Conversation 1

1. Where is Steven? _____

2. Does Mark know when Steven will be back? _____

3. Are Steven and Tina cousins? _____

4. What does Tina want Steven to do? _____

Conversation 2

1. Who's going to be fifty years old? _____

2. What time is the party? _____

3. Does Steven know where Café Roma is? _____

4. What shouldn't Steven bring to the party? _____

■ EXERCISE 4

A. *Write the questions in the correct order. Then compare with a partner.*

1. don't / a dictionary / do / you / you / have ___*You don't have a dictionary, do you*___?

2. go to bed / late / you / do / early / or _____?

3. this book / know / you / do / costs / how much _____?

4. kind of music / what / your / is / favorite _____?

5. family / you / a / big / have / do _____?

6. you / in / an apartment / a house / do / live / or _____?

7. you / this / me / what time / can / tell / finishes / class _____?

8. this weekend / doing / what / you / are _____?

9. drive / to class / don't / you / you _____?

10. next year / you / going to / are / graduate _____?

B. 🎧 *Listen and check your answers.*

C. *Work in a group. Ask and answer the questions in Exercise A.*

A: *You don't have a dictionary, do you?*

B: *Yes, actually, I have an electronic dictionary. Here you go.*

PUT IT TOGETHER

Small Talk

When people get together in informal social, business, or school situations, they often make "small talk." This might be at a party, before a meeting, on a train, or between classes. If the people are strangers, they want to learn a little about one another so they ask questions. Small-talk conversations can be about personal information or about everyday topics, such as the weather or sports.

■ EXERCISE 1

A. Vocabulary Preview *Match the words to their definitions. Use a dictionary if necessary. Then use the words to complete the sentences below.*

_____ 1. fantastic	a. a person who lives very close to you
_____ 2. neighbor	b. in the beginning
_____ 3. apartment complex	c. great; wonderful
_____ 4. accountant	d. a group of related buildings where people live
_____ 5. originally	e. a person who keeps track of costs and income

6. Do you live in a small apartment building or a big _____?

7. Jennifer is my new _____. She bought the house across the street.

8. If you start your own business, you should hire an _____ to take care of your finances.

9. I've lived in New York for the past ten years, but I'm _____ from India.

10. This is a _____ location for a resort hotel. It has beautiful views of both the mountains and the beach.

B. 🎧 *Listen to the small-talk conversation at a party. Check (✓) the topics the people talk about.*

☐ the weather   ☐ school

☐ their families   ☐ their jobs

☐ people they know   ☐ their hobbies

☐ where they live   ☐ their favorite foods

C. 🎧 *Listen and circle the best response to the question.*

1. a. Yes, it is. Thank you.

    b. I'm Grace. Grace Chang.

2. a. No, I prefer to be outdoors.

    b. Yeah. The weather's been great lately.

3. a. No, we don't.

    b. No. We went to university together.

4. a. I have an apartment not far from here.

    b. I'm originally from California.

5. a. Sure. It's just a couple of blocks from where I live.

    b. I don't think it's a very nice street.

6. a. The Cascades.

    b. No. I don't live there anymore.

7. a. It's Tina Jackson.

    b. No. I'm afraid I don't.

8. a. It's a big apartment complex.

    b. I lived in California until last month.

9. a. Oh, yeah. I've lived here all my life.

    b. No, it's not far. I usually take the bus.

10. a. Yes, he's a really nice guy.

    b. We were good friends as kids.

11. a. Yes, I can play both very well.

    b. Well, I prefer to play golf.

12. a. Sure, that would be great.

    b. My name's Grace.

D. *Read the small talk topics and questions. Write one more question for each topic. Then talk to three classmates. Ask each classmate about a different topic.*

Family

1. Are you an only child?
2. Do your grandparents live with you?
3. _____
   _____

Friends

1. Who is your best friend?
2. What do you like to do with your friends?
3. _____
   _____

School or work

1. Do you like school?
2. Do you have a job?
3. _____
   _____

Hobbies

1. What sports do you like?
2. Do you collect anything?
3. _____
   _____

Job Interview

Before hiring new employees, most employers interview them. Employers often ask questions to find out about personal information, job experience, educational background, and future goals.

■ EXERCISE 2

A. Vocabulary Preview *Read the sentences. Then circle the best definition for the underlined word(s).*

1. The manager read your <u>résumé</u>. She wants to ask you some questions about your last job.

   a. a book that one person writes about another person's life

   b. a document that includes information about your education and work experience

2. Last year, the team had an <u>impressive</u> record. In fact, they won every game they played.

   a. very good; admirable

   b. complete; thorough

3. Carla's going to college next year. She wants to <u>major in</u> English and become an English teacher.

   a. study as a main subject

   b. give up studying

4. I've worked at my company for six years. Next year, I hope to be a department <u>supervisor</u>.

   a. person who cleans buildings

   b. person who checks people's work; a manager

5. My boss has a difficult job. He has to make <u>decisions</u> about a lot of important things.

   a. choices

   b. stories

B. 🎧 *Listen to some questions you might hear at a job interview. Then circle the best response for each question.*

1. a. On the bus. How about you?

   b. Pretty well, thank you. How are you?

2. a. About six years.

   b. Yes, quite a bit.

3. a. No, actually, I didn't.

   b. I studied business.

4. a. Well, I worked in a bank for several years.

   b. Yes. I'm sure I'll be able to.

5. a. Yes, I do. I took several classes in college.

   b. Yes, I have. I took several classes in college.

6. a. My supervisor's name was Mr. Wilson.

   b. Yes. I was manager of a clothing store.

7. a. No. I haven't worked at any other companies.

   b. Well, I'd like to work for a small company.

8. a. Yes, I could.

   b. In two weeks.

9. a. Yes. I do have a few.

   b. Thank you so much.

C. 🎧 *Now listen to some common job interview questions. Answer with your own information.*

1. _____

2. _____

3. _____

4. _____

5. _____

6. _____

D. *With your class, think of more questions that an employer might ask someone looking for a job. Your teacher will write your ideas on the board. When you finish, choose five questions and interview a partner.*

Understanding Numbers

Unit Warm Up

Work with a partner. Look at the movie review blog. How do you say each movie title?

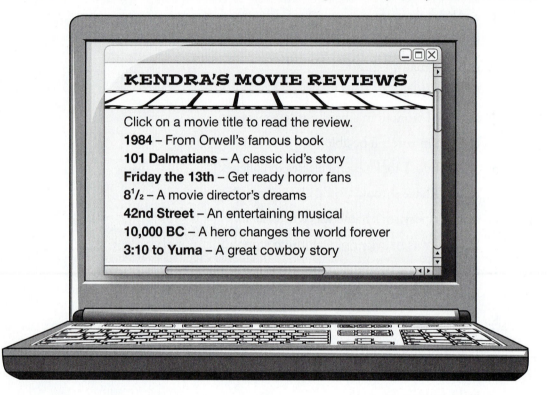

KENDRA'S MOVIE REVIEWS

Click on a movie title to read the review.
1984 – From Orwell's famous book
101 Dalmatians – A classic kid's story
Friday the 13th – Get ready horror fans
8$\frac{1}{2}$ – A movie director's dreams
42nd Street – An entertaining musical
10,000 BC – A hero changes the world forever
3:10 to Yuma – A great cowboy story

Example

A: The first one is nineteen eighty-four.

B: Right. And the second one is ...

SKILL PRESENTATION

We learn numbers and counting early in any language. It may not be difficult to count in English, but we do much more than simply count with numbers. We use numbers in many different ways: to talk about prices, phone numbers, addresses, dates, and telling time. It's important to learn the different ways numbers are used so that you can understand them when you hear them.

Ordinal Numbers

We use ordinal numbers to talk about items in a series.

🎧 *Listen and repeat the numbers.*

1st	first	**8th**	eighth	**40th**	fortieth
2nd	second	**9th**	ninth	**50th**	fiftieth
3rd	third	**10th**	tenth	**60th**	sixtieth
4th	fourth	**20th**	twentieth	**70th**	seventieth
5th	fifth	**21st**	twenty-first	**80th**	eightieth
6th	sixth	**22nd**	twenty-second	**90th**	ninetieth
7th	seventh	**30th**	thirtieth	**100th**	one hundredth

☑ Check Yourself

🎧 *Listen and write the ordinal numbers you hear.*

1. _____   2. _____   3. _____   4. _____   5. _____   6. _____

Dates

We also use ordinal numbers to talk about specific dates on the calendar. We express the years in different ways, depending on the number.

🎧 *Listen and repeat the dates and years.*

Dates

January 2nd	January second
March 23rd	March twenty-third
October 30th	October thirtieth
December 31st	December thirty-first

Years

1802	eighteen oh two
1989	nineteen eighty-nine
2008	two thousand (and) eight
2012	two thousand (and) twelve / twenty twelve

Note
- For years before 2000, we usually say the number in two parts:

Example

> *1789 = seventeen eighty-nine*   *1986 = nineteen eighty-six*

- We can use two different ways to talk about years after 2009:

Example

> *2011 = two thousand eleven*   or   *2011 = twenty eleven*

☑ **Check Yourself**

🎧 *Listen and write the dates and years.*

1. _____   4. _____
2. _____   5. _____
3. _____   6. _____

Addresses and Phone Numbers

We often need to understand addresses and phone numbers. If you misunderstand these numbers, it could mean going to the wrong place or calling the wrong phone number. It's especially important to know how these types of numbers are expressed so that you can avoid these kinds of mistakes.

🎧 *Listen and repeat the addresses and phone numbers.*

Addresses

303 Maple Lane	three oh three Maple Lane
5397 3rd Street	fifty-three ninety-seven Third Street
210 1st Avenue	two one zero First Avenue / two ten First Avenue

Phone Numbers

808-331-2546	eight oh eight, three three one, two five four six
515-547-2608	five one five, five four seven, two six oh eight
1-710-838-9020	one, seven one oh, eight three eight, nine oh two oh

Note
- For addresses, we usually express larger numbers in two parts (just like we do for years).

Example

> *911 Clark Avenue = nine eleven Clark Avenue*
> *1572 Main Street = fifteen seventy-two Main Street*

- For phone numbers, we say each number separately. We do not say the "-" symbol between the sets of numbers. We simply pause.

☑ **Check Yourself**

🎧 *Listen and write the correct addresses and phone numbers.*

Address

1. _____

2. _____

3. _____

Phone Number

4. _____

5. _____

6. _____

Expressions for Telling Time

Different English speakers may express the same time in different ways. This can be confusing when you are learning English. It's important to know all of the different ways for expressing time.

🎧 *Listen and repeat the times.*

10:00	ten / ten o'clock	**5:03**	five oh three
10:15	ten fifteen / a quarter past ten	**5:20**	five twenty
10:30	ten thirty / half past ten	**5:27**	five twenty-seven
10:45	ten forty-five / quarter to eleven	**5:55**	five fifty-five / five to six

☑ **Check Yourself**

🎧 *Listen to each sentence and write the time.*

1. __7:30__   2. _____   3. _____   4. _____   5. _____   6. _____

Prices

We need to understand prices when we ask how much something costs or when the clerk tells us how much we need to pay.

🎧 *Listen and repeat the prices.*

$ 2.00   two dollars
$ 3.50   three dollars (and) fifty cents / three fifty
$ 87.05   eighty-seven dollars (and) five cents / eight-seven oh five
$412.99   four hundred (and) twelve dollars (and) ninety-nine cents

> **Note**
> We always say *oh*—not *zero*—for the number "0" in prices:
>
> **Example**
> ·········
>
> *$27.05 = twenty-seven oh five*

☑ Check Yourself

🎧 *Listen and write the prices.*

1. ___$2.50___   4. _____
2. _____   5. _____
3. _____   6. _____

Temperatures

It's important to understand temperatures when we listen to a weather report or talk about science. *Fahrenheit* and *Celsius* are two different scales used to report temperatures.

🎧 *Listen and repeat the temperatures.*

32°   thirty-two degrees
212°F   two hundred (and) twelve degrees Fahrenheit
100°C   one hundred degrees Celsius
−40°   minus forty degrees / 40 degrees below zero / 40 below

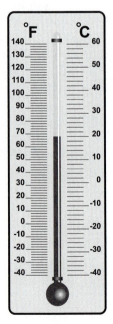

☑ **Check Yourself**

🎧 *Listen and circle the correct temperature.*

1. 37°C / 39°C
2. 96°F / 98.6°F
3. 0°F / 0°C

4. −128.6°F / 128.6°F
5. 107°C / 170°C

Fractions, Percentages, and Decimals

Fractions, percentages and decimals are especially important for students. These types of numbers are often found in lectures, research, or surveys.

🎧 *Listen and repeat.*

1/2	one-half / half	**50%**	fifty percent
1/3	one-third / a third	**100%**	one hundred percent
1/4	one-fourth / a fourth	**52.8%**	fifty-two point eight percent
2/3	two-thirds	**1.25%**	one point two five percent
3/4	three-fourths / three-quarters	**0.5%**	zero point five percent / half a percent

☑ **Check Yourself**

🎧 *Listen and write the fractions, percentages, and decimals.*

1. ____   2. ____   3. ____   4. ____   5. ____   6. ____

Large Numbers

Understanding large numbers in another language can be challenging. The expressions for larger numbers in English are often long and can be difficult to follow. You will build your understanding of large numbers with time and practice.

🎧 *Listen and repeat the numbers.*

100	a / one hundred	**201**	two hundred (and) one
1,000	a / one thousand	**4,306**	four thousand three hundred (and) six
10,000	ten thousand	**71,040**	seventy-one thousand forty
100,000	a / one hundred thousand	**994,000**	nine hundred ninety-four thousand
1,000,000	a / one million	**2,100,000**	two million one hundred thousand
1,000,000,000	a / one billion	**1,300,000,000**	one billion three hundred million

☑ Check Yourself

🎧 *Listen and write the numbers.*

1. _____   3. _____   5. _____

2. _____   4. _____   6. _____

PRACTICE

■ **EXERCISE 1**

A. 🎧 *Listen to each conversation and write the missing information.*

1. **Personal Information**
   Name: Suzanne Wilson
   Address: _____
       Los Angeles, California
   Date of birth: _____
   Phone: _____ (cell)

2. **Price**
   jacket: _____
   blouse: _____
   skirt: _____
   belt: _____

3. **Temperatures**

   Paris: _____

   London: _____

   Berlin: _____

   Copenhagen: _____

   Milan: _____

4. **Times**

   start work: _____

   finish work: _____

   see cousin: _____

   doctor's appointment: _____

   meet Jeff: _____

5. **Phone Numbers**

   home: _____

   cell: _____

   work: _____

6. **Large Numbers**

   1990: _____

   2000: _____

   2010: _____

B. 🎧 *Listen again. Answer the questions.*

   1. How much does the class cost? _____

   2. How much lower is the skirt price? _____

   3. What time is the next weather update? _____

   4. What's the man's extension? _____

   5. What times does the movie start? _____

   6. What's the population this year? _____

■ **EXERCISE 2**

A. *Work with a partner. Take turns reading the sentences.*

   1. Both of my parents were born in 1962.

   2. 1/2 of 1/4 is 1/8, isn't it?

   3. Today's date is May 21st.

   4. She was born in 1992.

   5. The city's population is 12,146,900.

   6. He lives at 2037 Maple Lane.

   7. My cell phone number is 427-555-0912.

   8. This shirt is on sale for $13.49.

   9. I'll meet you at the restaurant at 11:45.

   10. Her new salary is now $58,500 a year.

   11. The temperature outside is −12°C.

   12. Prices increased last year by only 0.35%.

B. *Cross out and change all of the numbers in Exercise A. Then read your new sentences. Your partner writes the new numbers.*

1. _____ 5. _____ 9. _____

2. _____ 6. _____ 10. _____

3. _____ 7. _____ 11. _____

4. _____ 8. _____ 12. _____

C. *Check your partner's numbers. Are they correct?*

■ **EXERCISE 3**

Work in a group. Discuss the questions.

1. What emergency phone numbers do you know?

   What are the numbers?

   What other phone numbers do you have memorized?

2. When were you born?

   When were your parents born?

3. What's your address?

   What other addresses of places do you know?

4. What time do you usually get up?

   What time do you usually go to bed?

5. What do you think the temperature is right now?

   What do you think the temperature will be tonight?

6. About how many people live in your country?

   About how many live in its largest city?

7. What's the best university in your country?

   About how many students go there?

PUT IT TOGETHER

A Record Number of Records

The book *Guinness World Records* is a reference book that lists world records in many fields. For example, it lists the oldest person, the tallest person, the faster runner, the most expensive car, and many other records. Some of the records are a little strange. One man—Ashrita Furman—holds many of these records.

■ **EXERCISE 1**

A. Vocabulary Preview *Read the sentences below. Then match the underlined words to their correct definitions.*

_____ 1. Wow! I can't believe you won the marathon. That's <u>incredible</u>!

_____ 2. I'd like to visit Madrid. I'm <u>fascinated</u> by Spanish culture.

_____ 3. Tim is the fastest swimmer on the team. He <u>set a record</u> for the 100 meters.

_____ 4. Karen wants to be an art teacher. She hopes to <u>inspire</u> children to be creative.

_____ 5. The Eiffel Tower and Notre Dame Cathedral are two famous Paris <u>landmarks</u>.

_____ 6. It's Vivian's birthday. We need sixteen <u>candles</u> for the cake.

_____ 7. How many times can you <u>bounce</u> a soccer ball on your knees?

_____ 8. Jun Hee can play guitar and sing, but he can't do both <u>simultaneously</u>.

a. famous buildings or sights

b. make someone want to do something

c. at the same time

d. hit a ball so that it goes up and down

e. difficult to believe; amazing

f. sticks of wax with a piece of string that burns on one end

g. to do something faster or more times than anyone else

h. very interested in

B. 🎧 *Listen to the information about Ashrita Furman. Write answers to the questions.*

1. When was Ashrita Furman born? _____

2. In what year did he join the bike race in New York's Central Park?

   _____

3. How far did he ride? _____

4. In what place did he finish the race (first, second, etc.)? _____

5. How many jumping jacks did he do for his first record? _____

6. What two records did he set in 1986?

   a. did forward rolls along a _____ route in Boston

   b. jumped _____ miles on Mount Fuji in Japan

Understanding Numbers   **23**

C. 🎧 *Listen and complete the chart.*

Date	Event	Record
1. August _____	underwater rope jumping	completed _____ rope jumps without stopping
2. November _____	grape catching	caught _____ grapes in _____ minutes
3. July _____	candles on a cake	_____ candles
4. March _____	pushing a car	_____ miles (_____ kilometers) in _____ hours
5. February _____	basketball bouncing	_____ bounces in one minute
6. April _____, 2009	world records	first person to hold _____ records simultaneously; has broken records in _____ different countries

D. **Work in a group. Try to set some records. See who can ...**

- balance this book on his or her head the longest.
- stand on one foot the longest.
- name all of the students in the class the fastest.
- jump the farthest.
- fly a paper airplane the farthest.

The Vocabulary of English

The English language has a large, rich, and growing vocabulary, much of which has been taken from other languages. In this talk, you will hear some information about the vocabulary of English.

■ **EXERCISE 2**

A. **Vocabulary Preview** *Study the words and their definitions. Then use the words to complete the sentences on the next page.*

conquer	to take land by force; to occupy
typically	generally; usually
linguist	a person who studies language
specialized	suitable for one specific purpose
informal	suitable for ordinary language

1. The _____ is studying the grammar of several ancient languages.

2. Children _____ begin speaking at between 12 to 24 months of age.

3. The Romans were able to _____ all the lands around the Mediterranean Sea.

4. Spoken language is generally more _____ than written language.

5. This is a highly _____ tool. It has only one use.

B. 🎧 *Listen to the talk about English vocabulary and write the missing numbers.*

A language called "Old English" was spoken in most parts of Britain from the _____ century to the _____ century. It is believed that Old English contained from about _____ to _____ words. In the year _____, Britain was conquered by the French, and many French words were added to the language. During the _____ and _____ centuries, many words were added from other European languages, such as Spanish and Portuguese, and from far-away places in the Americas, Africa, and Asia. Even today, languages continue to borrow from one another.

Today, some linguists believe that the English language may contain _____ words, although no one person knows that many words. Probably more than _____ of these words are specialized words—words that would be used only in certain fields, such as medicine or engineering.

By the age of five or six, an English-speaking child knows from about _____ to _____ words. During the early years of elementary school, an average student learns from _____ to _____ words a year, or from two to eight a day. Among adult speakers of English, the size of a person's vocabulary varies greatly. A study done in _____ indicated that a high-school graduate has an average of about _____ words and that a person with a university degree typically has a vocabulary of around _____ words.

A _____ study found that it is not necessary for nonnative speakers to have a large vocabulary in order to understand a lot of spoken or written English. According to the study, a person with a vocabulary of just _____ of the most common words can understand about _____ percent of an informal conversation. A person with a vocabulary of _____ words can understand _____ percent of a written text.

C. *Work with a partner. Guess the answers to the World Languages quiz. Check your answers at the bottom of the page.*

Example

> *A: I think the answer to question one is five hundred and seventeen.*
>
> *B: Really? I'm not sure. I think it's ...*

World Languages Quiz

1. About how many languages are spoken in the world?

   a. 500

   b. 7,000

   c. 10,000

2. How many people are native English speakers?

   a. between 30,000,000 and 40,000,000

   b. between 75,000,000 and 80,000,000

   c. between 300,000,000 and 500,000,000

3. How long have languages existed?

   a. since about 500 BCE

   b. since about 2,000 BCE

   c. since about 10,000 BCE

4. About how many languages are spoken in Papua New Guinea (the country with the most languages in the world)?

   a. 120

   b. 850

   c. 2,000

5. When was the first language (Sumerian) written?

   a. about 1500 BCE

   b. about 2000 BCE

   c. about 3200 BCE

6. Khmer, the language of Cambodia, has the largest alphabet. How many letters does it have ?

   a. 74

   b. 112

   c. 206

7. How many people are native speakers of Mandarin Chinese?

    a. .5 billion

    b. 1.1 billion

    c. 3.2 billion

8. In about how many countries is English an official language?

    a. 6

    b. 60

    c. 600

1.b 2.c 3.c 4.b 5.c 6.a 7.b 8.b

Answers

Understanding Reduced Forms

Unit Warm Up

Work with a partner. Read these song titles aloud. What are the reduced (short) forms? What are their full forms?

Now Playing

Sheryl Crow – All I Wanna Do

Alanis Morissette - You Oughta Know

Pink - 'Cuz I Can

Britney Spears Gimme More

Stevie Wonder - I Gotta Have a Song

Led Zeppelin - Rock 'n' Roll

| Songs | Artists | Albums | Videos | More |

MENU

SKILL PRESENTATION

English-speakers often use the reduced (short) forms of words in daily speech. It's not necessary to use these short forms yourself, but it is important to understand them We usually do not write reduced forms, but you may see some of them in songs, advertisements, and informal personal writing. There are many different types of reduced forms in English. This section will give you practice listening to and understanding some of the most common reduced forms.

Greetings

We often use reduced forms for greetings, especially when we say hello or goodbye to friends in casual situations.

🎧 *Listen and repeat the full forms and their reduced forms.*

Saying Hello		Saying Goodbye	
1. How are you?	howarya	**1.** See you.	seeya
2. How's it going?	howzitgoin	**2.** Goodbye	g'bye

Remember

We do not usually use reduced forms in writing. In this book, they are written to help you see how the reduced forms are pronounced.

☑ Check Yourself

Practice the greetings. Say hello to three classmates. Have a short conversation. Then say goodbye. Try to use reduced forms.

Short Words and Phrases with *Me* and *To*

Some of the most common reduced forms include short words like *and* and *of*, as well as phrases with *me* and *to*.

🎧 *Listen and repeat the full forms and their reduced forms.*

Short Words	
1. and	n
2. of	uh
3. them	em
4. because	cuz

Verb + me	
1. give me	gimme
2. let me	lemme

Verb or Modal + to	
1. want to	wanna
2. going to	gonna
3. has to	hasta
4. have to	hafta
5. got to	gotta
6. ought to	oughta

🎧 *Listen. Does the speaker use the reduced form or the full form of the words in bold? Check (✓) your answer.*

	Reduced Form	Full Form
1. I had juice, eggs, **and** some bread for breakfast.	☐	☐
2. Are all **of** your friends coming to the party?	☐	☐
3. Did Ryan tell **them** to come on time?	☐	☐
4. Please **let me** see your paper.	☐	☐
5. Can you **give me** your phone number again?	☐	☐
6. Are you **going to** go home right after class?	☐	☐
7. I have **got to** get a haircut soon.	☐	☐
8. Paul and Gina **have to** work Saturday night.	☐	☐

Question Forms

We often use reduced form with questions, especially with *Wh-* questions and the pronoun *you*.

🎧 *Listen and repeat the full forms and their reduced forms.*

1.	Don't you	doncha	8.	What did you	whadja
2.	Did you	didja	9.	Where did you	wheredja
3.	Didn't you	didncha	10.	Who did you	whodja
4.	Would you	wouldja	11.	When did you	whendja
5.	Could you	couldja	12.	How did you	howdja
6.	What do you	whadaya	13.	Why did you	whydja
7.	What are you	whatcha			

A. 🎧 *Listen and complete the questions. Write the full forms.*

1. _____ lend me your dictionary?

2. _____ doing this weekend?

3. _____ spell your last name?

4. _____ know my cell phone number?

5. _____ send me an email message yesterday?

6. _____ do last night?

7. _____ get here?

8. _____ join this class?

B. *Work with a partner. Ask and answer the questions in Exercise A. Use reduced forms.*

PRACTICE

■ EXERCISE 1

🎧 *Listen. Does the speaker use reduced forms? Check (✓) Yes or No.*

	Yes	No
1. How's it going?	☐	☐
2. My brother and sister are both in college.	☐	☐
3. Do you have to study this weekend?	☐	☐
4. Why didn't you tell your mother the truth?	☐	☐
5. Where did you go to high school?	☐	☐
6. Do you want to see a movie with me sometime?	☐	☐
7. I was late this morning because the bus was late.	☐	☐
8. My parents called but I haven't called them back.	☐	☐
9. What are you listening to?	☐	☐
10. Did you watch the news last night?	☐	☐

■ EXERCISE 2

🎧 *Listen. Underline any reduced forms you hear.*

1. <u>How are you</u>? It's really great to see you again.
2. Would you ever travel alone? I don't think I would.
3. When did you and your parents move to this neighborhood?
4. Don't you remember me? I was in your English class last year.
5. Our teacher has to leave early today, so we have a short class.
6. How did you get my number? Did someone give it to you?
7. Where did you get that dress? I really like it.
8. I've got to go away this weekend. Do you want to come with me?
9. What are you doing? Do you want to take a walk?
10. What do you do on the weekend? Do you have a part-time job?
11. I have to make a quick call. Could you lend me your phone?
12. I'm going to stay home and study tonight because I have to take a test tomorrow.

■ EXERCISE 3

🎧 *Listen to each question. Check (✓) the best answer.*

1. a ☐ Sure. I'd love to.   b ☐ In the morning.
2. a ☐ Very well, thank you.   b ☐ P-A-R-K.
3. a ☐ It's my sister's.   b ☐ $25.99.
4. a ☐ I went to school.   b ☐ Nothing much.
5. a ☐ Sure. How much?   b ☐ Yes, I did.
6. a ☐ I'm going to the library.   b ☐ I visited my parents.
7. a ☐ Yes, I am.   b ☐ Yes, I did.
8. a ☐ My brother.   b ☐ A sandwich.
9. a ☐ I took a bus.   b ☐ I got a 90.
10. a ☐ No, I don't.   b ☐ No, I didn't.

A. 🎧 *Listen and complete each conversation. Write the full forms.*

Conversation 1

Jennifer: Hi, Michael. How's it going?

Michael: Oh, hi Jennifer. Not bad. How are you?

Jennifer: Pretty good. _____ doing?

Michael: I'm just going to the library.

Jennifer: How come?

Michael: Because I have to study.

Jennifer: Why didn't you study last night?

Michael: I don't know. I always wait until the last minute.

Jennifer: _____ doing later? Do you _____ get together?

Michael: OK. _____ a call around five o'clock _____ we can make plans.

Jennifer: Sounds good.

Conversation 2

Tina: How was your trip to Mexico, Sarah?

Sarah: It was fantastic! But it was too short. I was only there for a week.

Tina: _____ get back?

Sarah: Last Saturday.

Tina: _____ go exactly?

Sarah: Mexico City and Cancún.

Tina: Nice! _____ like Cancún?

Sarah: I loved it. Do you _____ see my photos when I get _____?

Tina: Sure! And _____ travel with?

Sarah: My sister.

Conversation 3

Terry: Hello.

Wendy: Terry? Hi, it's Wendy.

Terry: Hey, Wendy! _____ doing?

Wendy: Not much. I wanted to ask you about Mr. Mason's class today. _____ go?

Terry: I did. He presented some new material but it was _____ boring.

Wendy: _____ see your notes?

Terry: I guess so. But _____ miss the class?

(continued)

Wendy: I was up until one o'clock _____ I just overslept.

Terry: Listen, I've _____ go. I have another call.

Wendy: Oh, OK. _____ later.

B. *Practice the conversations in Exercise A with a partner. Try to use reduced forms.*

■ EXERCISE 5

A. *Complete these questions with your own ideas.*

1. Did you _____ ?
2. Where did you _____ ?
3. What are you _____ ?
4. Do you have to _____ ?
5. Could you _____ ?
6. When did you _____ ?
7. What do you _____ ?
8. How did you _____ ?
9. Are you going to _____ ?
10. Do you want to _____ ?

B. *Practice asking your questions from Exercise A. Try to use reduced forms.*

C. *Now work with a partner. Ask and answer your questions. Use reduced forms.*

Example

A: Did you watch TV last night?

B: No. I played video games.

■ EXERCISE 6

A. *Walk around the class. Ask yes/no questions. If someone answers yes, write the person's name in the first column. Then ask a Wh- question to complete the last column.*

Find someone who ...	Name	Additional information
has to work this weekend.		
bought some new clothes last week.		
is going to go shopping after class.		
wants to travel overseas.		
has to study tonight.		

cooked dinner last night.		
went out of town last weekend.		
would like to go out for coffee later.		

Example

A: Do you have to work this weekend?

B: Yes, I do.

A: And where do you work?

B. **Tell the class the most interesting information from your chart in Exercise A.**

PUT IT TOGETHER

Strange Inventions

Every year, there are thousands of new inventions. Some of these inventions become popular and make a lot of money for their inventors. Some of them fail, and some of them are just strange. In this section, you will hear about an inventions contest. A judge is interviewing inventors about their inventions.

■ EXERCISE 1

A. Vocabulary Preview *Read each sentence. Then circle the best definition for the underlined word(s).*

1. My home is small and simple. It's just an <u>ordinary</u> house.

    a. beautiful   b. plain

2. No, thank you. I don't need any dessert. I don't want to <u>gain weight</u>.

    a. become heavier   b. become strong

3. I fell down in front of all those people. It was so <u>embarrassing</u>.

    a. causing social discomfort   b. causing sickness

4. Laptop computers are very <u>practical</u>. They're small and light, and you can take them anywhere.

    a. convenient   b. confusing

5. Oh, no! I spilled dirt everywhere in the kitchen. Do you have a <u>vacuum cleaner</u>?

    a. machine for washing clothes   b. machine for cleaning the floor

6. These books are very, very old. They're all covered with <u>dust</u>.

    a. very small pieces of dirt   b. photos and drawings

(continued)

7. Today our cooking teacher is going to <u>demonstrate</u> how to bake French bread.

    a. show   b. study

8. Jack is a very <u>clever</u> boy. He's always full of good ideas.

    a. intelligent   b. shy

B. 🎧 *Listen and complete the conversation. Write the full forms. Then compare your answers with a partner.*

Invention: The Alarm Fork

Judge: OK. We're here with our first inventor, Rick Kowalski. Hello, Rick.

Rick: Hi. _____(1)_____?

Judge: Great, thanks. So, _____(2)_____ have here? It looks like a … a fork.

Rick: Yes, but this is no ordinary fork. It's an alarm fork!

Judge: Interesting … _____(3)_____ tell us about it? _____(4)_____ create the alarm fork?

Rick: Well, everybody knows it's not healthy to eat too fast, right? When you eat too fast, you eat too much, _____(5)_____ you gain weight. Also, when you eat too fast, you don't really enjoy your food, _____(6)_____ you don't really taste it. I think people _____(7)_____ slow down and enjoy their food. For a lot of people, meals are the only time they spend with their families—the only time they get to talk to _____(8)_____, so you don't want mealtime to go too fast.

Judge: Yes, I suppose that's all true. _____(9)_____ explain how it works?

Rick: Sure, _____(10)_____ show you. You see this little green light? That means you can take a bite _____(11)_____ food. Here, take a bite of this chocolate cake.

Judge: Oh, don't mind if I do … Mmm. That's good. Thank you.

Rick: Now, you see. The light on the fork is red. You _____(12)_____ wait thirty seconds before you take another bite.

Judge: I do? What if I don't _____ wait? What's _____
(13)   (14)

happen if I take a bite when the light's still red?

Rick: Why _____ take a bite and see?
(15)

Judge: All right ... Whoa!! I guess that could be a little embarrassing at a dinner

party. Well, Rick Kowalski—a very practical invention. Thanks a lot for

showing it to us.

Rick: My pleasure. _____.
(16)

C. 🎧 *Listen and complete the conversation. Write the full forms. Then compare your answers with a partner.*

Invention: The Laptop Vacuum

Judge: Now here with our second inventor, Kim Richards. Hi, Kim.

Kim: Hi. _____?
(1)

Judge: Good thanks. Is this your invention? It looks like a ... a tiny vacuum

cleaner. _____ call it?
(2)

Kim: I call it the laptop vacuum.

Judge: Uh huh ... I see. And _____ get the idea for this invention?
(3)

Kim: Well, _____ ever notice those tiny pieces _____
(4)   (5)

dirt and dust that get down inside your computer keyboard?

Judge: Yeah. Sometimes I eat while I'm working on the computer, and little bits

_____ food fall down in there. I have no idea how to get
(6)

_____ out!
(7)

(continued)

Kim: Well, that's what my invention is for—cleaning up your laptop.

Judge: Great idea! _____ mind demonstrating how it works?
(8)

Kim: Here, you've really _____ try it for yourself. Just plug this cord
(9)

into this computer .... and start vacuuming.

Judge: Hey, that's pretty clever. I'll bet this is _____ be a popular
(10)

item once it hits the stores.

Kim: Oh, thank you. I hope so!

D. *Work in a group. Follow these instructions:*

1. Discuss: Which invention from Exercises B and C do you think should win the contest? Why?

2. One of the inventions discussed in Exercises B and C is real. (You can buy it in stores and online.) Which one do you think it is?

3. With your group members, create an invention to enter in the contest. Then describe it to the class. Explain the following:

   - What it is   • How it works
   - Who it's for   • Why it's useful
   - What it does

Example
....

Our invention is dishwasher gloves. It's for ...

UNIT 4 Understanding Homonyms

Unit Warm Up

Work with a partner. Read the riddles. Do you understand them? What makes them funny?

Q: What do you call a grizzly with no clothes?

A: *A bare bear.*

Q: What has four wheels and flies?

A: *A garbage truck.*

SKILL PRESENTATION

Homonyms are words that sound or look alike. There are two types of homonyms:

- **Homophones:** Words that sound alike but have different spellings, like *bear* (a large animal) and *bare* (uncovered) in the first joke above.

- **Homographs:** Words that are spelled the same but have different meanings, like two meanings of the word *flies* (insects) and *flies* (travels through the air) in the second joke.

These words can sometimes be confusing when you are learning English. In this unit, you will practice listening and understanding the differences between both types of homonyms.

Common Homonyms

Here are some examples of common homonyms in English.

Read the list of homonyms.

bored / board	hear / here	wait / weight
fare / fair	passed / past	weather / whether
flour / flower	red / read	we'll / wheel
flew / flu	vary / very	who's / whose

> **Note**
> Because many homonyms sound exactly the same, you can use the context (the other words in the sentence or conversation) to know which word the speaker is using. For example, when you hear *I need some flour. I'm baking a cake,* you can guess that the word is *flour* and not *flower.* The context of *baking* gives you a big clue. The word *some* also helps because *flowers* would have to be plural after *some.*

☑ Check Yourself

A. 🎧 *Listen and circle the word you hear.*

1. a. flour   b. flower
2. a. bored   b. board
3. a. wait   b. weight
4. a. fare   b. fair
5. a. who's   b. whose
6. a. here   b. hear

7. a. weather   b. whether
8. a. flew   b. flu
9. a. very   b. vary
10. a. we'll   b. wheel
11. a. read   b. red
12. a. past   b. passed

B. **Work with a partner. Write a homonym for each word. Use a dictionary if necessary. Then check your answers with your teacher.**

ad	hole	sail
ate	hour	seen
bury	it's	son
blew	knows	tail
buy	mail	vary
scent	meet	waist
dye	maid	weight
due	new	wear

eye	one	weak
fair	pear	wood
fined	past	write
flu	piece	you're
for	plain	their, there
guest	red	to, too
hi	roll	

C. Work in groups. Are there any words you don't know in Exercise B? Review the list together to make sure you know all the meanings.

PRACTICE

■ EXERCISE 1

🎧 *Read each conversation. Complete the sentences with homonyms from the Skill Presentation section. Then listen and check your answers.*

1.

 A: Would you like a sandwich?

 B: No, thank you. I already _____.

2.

 A: Do you usually take the bus to school?

 B: Yes. The _____ is only a dollar.

3.

 A: How old is your daughter?

 B: She's seven. She'll be _____ in a few weeks.

4.

 A: How was the movie last night?

 B: Well, I enjoyed it, but Greg didn't. He said he was _____.

5.

 A: How did you do in the basketball game on Saturday?

 B: Great! My team _____ by sixteen points!

6.

 A: Would anyone like this last piece of cake?

 B: OK. I'll eat it. I don't want to _____ it.

(continued)

7.

    A: How do you like this jacket?

    B: It's a little _____. I prefer this one. It's more colorful.

8.

    A: Do you want to go out to dinner tonight?

    B: Oh, I'd love to, but I have to work until seven.

    A: That's OK. I can _____. We can go when you finish work.

■ EXERCISE 2

Work with a partner. Complete the puzzle with words from the list on page xx.

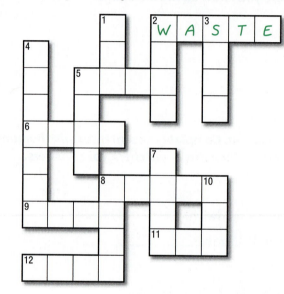

Across

2. not save
5. past of *make*
6. found at the end of some animals
8. a piece of wood
9. small round bread
11. You see with this.
12. not there

Down

1. a large body of water
2. Sunday to Sunday
3. a low price
4. rain, snow, wind, etc.
5. letters and packages
7. without clothes
8. a color
10. it colors your hair

■ EXERCISE 3

A. 🎧 *Listen to each conversation and write the missing words.*

Conversation 1

A: Is it time to _____ the _____?

B: Not yet. We just need to _____ a few more minutes.

A: Which gate are we leaving from?

B: That _____.

A: And _____ is Rick? He should be _____.

B: Who _____? Maybe he's at the bookstore.

A: Do you _____ when _____ arrive in Miami?

B: At about _____. I hope the _____ is nice in Florida.

A: Me _____. I really need some _____.

Conversation 2

A: What a _____!

B: I'm so glad _____ Friday.

A: What are you doing this weekend?

B: First I need to wash my clothes. I have nothing to _____. Then tomorrow afternoon I'm going shopping. There's a _____ cool _____ of shoes on _____ at Ace Department Store that I want to _____. How about you?

A: A friend from college is _____. He _____ in yesterday so _____ probably get together tomorrow night. Hey, _____ you like _____ join us?

B: Sure, thanks!

B. *Work with a partner. Practice the conversations in Exercise A.*

Remember

There are two types of homonyms:
- **homophones:** words that are spelled differently but sound the same
- **homographs:** words that are spelled the same but have different meanings

Read the two sentences. Circle the one word that could complete both sentences.

1. Lift this chair. It's really _____.

   I can't see a thing. Can you turn on the _____?

   a. lamp   b. light   c. heavy   d. match

2. Someone threw a _____ through her window? How awful!

   My favorite kind of music is _____.

   a. stone   b. jazz   c. rock   d. brick

3. Do you think anyone will ever _____ the *Titanic*?

   You're doing a fantastic job. You should ask for a _____.

   a. raise   b. lift   c. pay   d. office

4. The flight is going to _____ soon.

   The sailors haven't been on _____ in three weeks.

   a. fly   b. land   c. sand   d. close

5. I can't find my _____. Do you have the time?

   Let's get together and _____ TV tonight.

   a. clock   b. phone   c. record   d. watch

6. I think I'd like to _____ my hair color.

   Do you have any _____? Just a couple of coins?

   a. cents   b. cash   c. change   d. dye

7. Let's get the _____. Where's the waiter?

   Would you _____ my phone? It's not working.

   a. order   b. bill   c. fix   d. check

8. Can you help me with this problem? It doesn't seem _____.

   After you get to the bank, go _____.

   a. correct   b. right   c. left   d. straight

9. The new king has proven to be an excellent _____.

   I need a _____ so I can draw a straight line.

   a. guide   b. edge   c. leader   d. ruler

10. She's very famous. She even has her own _____ club.

    Do you want to turn on the _____ or the air conditioner?

    a. fan   b. heat   c. ice   d. web

■ **EXERCISE 5**

🎧 *Listen for the boldfaced word in the conversations. Check (✓) the meaning that matches how the word is used.*

1. **bank**   a ☐ the side of a river   b ☐ a building to keep money in

2. **box**   a ☐ a container   b ☐ to fight with your hands

3. **fast**   a ☐ quickly   b ☐ to go without food

4. **long**   a ☐ the opposite of short   b ☐ to hope for

5. **season**   a ☐ a time of year   b ☐ to add flavor to food

6. **staff**   a ☐ employees   b ☐ a walking stick

7. **state**   a ☐ a condition   b ☐ to say clearly

8. **tip**   a ☐ the end of something sharp   b ☐ to push or fall over

9. **last**   a ☐ the most recent or final   b ☐ to go on for a length of time

10. **key**   a ☐ something that opens a door   b ☐ something very important

11. **head**   a ☐ to move toward something   b ☐ the top part of a person's body

12. **fall**   a ☐ to drop down to the ground   b ☐ between summer and winter

13. **table**   a ☐ a chart of facts or figures   b ☐ a piece of furniture

14. **express**   a ☐ to state in words   b ☐ very fast

15. **upset**   a ☐ to win unexpectedly   b ☐ to make someone nervous

■ **EXERCISE 6**

A. 🎧 *Work in groups. Read each riddle and write the correct answer from the box (There are four extra answers.) Then listen and check your guesses.*

a telephone	week days	short days	stories
a hamburger	ate nine	books	fans
sunglasses	catch cold	Hawaii	a tennis ball

1. **Q:** Why are movie stars always so cool?

   A: Because they have so many _____.

2. **Q:** What can you serve but never eat?

   A: _____.

3. **Q:** Why are Saturday and Sunday the strongest days?

   A: Because the other days are_____.

4. **Q:** What has a ring but no finger?

   A: _____.

(continued)

5. **Q:** Which is faster, cold or heat?

    A: Heat, because you can _____.

6. **Q:** Why is the number 6 afraid of the number 7?

    A: Because seven _____.

7. **Q:** What is the tallest building in town?

    A: The library, because it has so many _____.

8. **Q:** What has two eyes that are very close together, but cannot see?

    A: The word _____.

B. *Talk with your group. What is the homonym in each riddle?*

PUT IT TOGETHER

In a Big-Box Store

"Big-box" stores are large stores that sell all kinds of things. Some people like going to big-box stores because they can do all their shopping in one store and because the prices are usually reasonable.

■ EXERCISE 1

A. Vocabulary Preview *Match the words to their definitions. Use a dictionary if necessary.*

_____ 1. huge   a. things inside a house (tables, chairs, etc.)

_____ 2. furniture   b. to give something and get something different in return; to trade

_____ 3. exchange   c. very, very large

_____ 4. jewelry   d. machines like computers, televisions, MP3 players, etc.

_____ 5. electronics   e. a place that sells medicine

_____ 6. pharmacy   f. a note from a doctor that tells what kind and how much medicine you need

_____ 7. prescription   g. rings, necklaces, bracelets, etc.

Remember

Use the context of the conversation to help you decide the correct homonyms.

B. 🎧 *Read the homonyms. Then listen to the conversation. Check (✓) the correct homonyms you hear.*

1. ☐ wear ☐ where
   ☐ sail ☐ sale
   ☐ pair ☐ pear
   ☐ waist ☐ waste

2. ☐ fined ☐ find
   ☐ scene ☐ seen
   ☐ wood ☐ would
   ☐ for ☐ four
   ☐ buy ☐ by

3. ☐ hi ☐ high
   ☐ whole ☐ hole
   ☐ right ☐ write
   ☐ wood ☐ would
   ☐ knew ☐ new
   ☐ blew ☐ blue

4. ☐ its ☐ it's
   ☐ where ☐ wear
   ☐ passed ☐ past
   ☐ ate ☐ eight
   ☐ our ☐ hour

5. ☐ do ☐ due
   ☐ flew ☐ flu
   ☐ write ☐ right
   ☐ seen ☐ scene
   ☐ weight ☐ wait

C. *Choose the correct homonyms from the box to complete each conversation.*

> change   watch   check   light   fan

Conversation 1

Customer: I bought this _____ here last week, and it doesn't keep the
                     (1)
correct time. I'd like to have it repaired.

Clerk: OK. I just need to _____ your receipt.
                     (2)

Customer: Here you are.

Clerk: Thanks. OK. First, I'm going to _____ the battery. I have a
                     (3)
new one right here.

Customer: Good idea. I didn't think of that.

Clerk: Well, it's working again. It looks like that was the problem. *(continued)*

Conversation 2

Wife: It's really hot in here. We need to buy a _____.
                                                                                  (4)

Husband: Yeah. Let's get one today. Jim and Joe are coming over to

_____ the baseball game tonight.
            (5)

Wife: I didn't know Joe was a baseball _____ ... OK. Let's go
                                                                          (6)

shopping at Merv's this afternoon.

Husband: Do I have to go?

Wife: Well, I might need help carrying the fan to the car.

Husband: You'll be OK – just, buy a _____ one!
                                                            (7)

Wife: Oh, all right. You don't have to come. But you do have to pay for it. I

think they cost around $40.00.

Husband: Great. Here's fifty. Could you buy some snacks with the

_____?
    (8)

Grocery List

■ EXERCISE 2

Experts say that when you go grocery shopping, you should always make a list of the foods that you need to buy. It will help you save time and money.

A. Vocabulary Preview *Read the conversations. Then circle the best definition for the underlined word(s).*

1. **A:** The weather is supposed to be really nice this weekend.

   B: Great! Let's have a <u>barbecue</u>. I'll bring the burgers.

      A *barbecue* is _____

      a. a sports competition

      b. an indoor party

      c. an event when people cook outdoors

2. **A:** Are you ready to order, sir?

   B: Yes. I think I'll just have the salad. I'm a <u>vegetarian</u>.

   > A *vegetarian* is someone who _____
   > a. takes care of animals
   > b. doesn't eat meat
   > c. works at a restaurant

3. **A:** Have you seen Wendy recently?

   B: Yes, she looks a little thinner. Is she <u>on a diet</u>?

   > Someone who is *on a diet* is _____
   > a. trying to lose weight
   > b. difficult to talk to
   > c. moving to a new place

4. **A:** I hope you enjoyed your meal.

   B: Yes, thank you. You're a wonderful cook. Everything was <u>delicious</u>.

   > *Delicious* means _____
   > a. too expensive
   > b. strange and unusual
   > c. having a very good taste

B. 🎧 *Complete the conversation with the correct homonyms from the box. Then listen and check your answers.*

ate / eight	meat / meet	to / too / two
flour / flower	one / won	wait / weight
guessed / guest	peace / piece	weak / week
hole / whole	know / no	whose / who's

Wife: So, before we go to the supermarket, let's make a list.

Husband: All right, sure.

Wife: Keep in mind that we're going to have a _____ for dinner
(1)
Sunday night.

Husband: Oh, really? _____ that?
(2)

(continued)

Wife: Oh, come on. I told you last _____. My Aunt Gladys is
                                    (3)
coming.

Husband: Oh, right. Well, let's just have a barbecue … We can grill some burgers in the

backyard.

Wife: You know Aunt Gladys doesn't eat _____! She's a
                                          (4)
vegetarian.

Husband: I didn't _____ that. I thought she _____
                   (5)   **(6)**
everything! Oh, well, you can make that vegetable dish that everyone likes.

Wife: Yeah—or maybe I should just get a nice _____ of fresh fish.
                                                    (7)
Yes, that's what I'll do. And we'll need a side dish.

Husband: Just _____? That isn't much food.
                (8)

Wife: Hmm. You're right. Maybe we'll need _____ side dishes.
                                                (9)

Husband: And if you get some _____, I could make a pie for dessert.
                                (10)

Wife: Mmm, that would be good. I can't have any though. I'm on a diet …

Husband: Oh, come on. You don't have to eat the _____ pie. Just a little
                                                    (11)
won't make you gain _____.
                    (12)

Wife: Oh, OK. You do make a delicious pie. I guess I can have a little.

Husband: All right, well, let's take the list and go shopping.

C. *Work with a partner. Write your own conversation. Use at least five homonyms from the box in Exercise B. Practice the conversation. Then present it to the class.*

Unit Warm Up

A. *Work with a partner. Read the proverbs. What do you think each one means? Match the proverbs to the pictures.*

a. Like father, like son.

b. Oil and water don't mix.

c. Out of sight, out of mind.

d. When the cat's away, the mice will play.

1. ☐

2. ☐

3. ☐

4. ☐

B. *Listen. Which words in each proverb does the speaker stress (say a little more strongly)? Underline them. Then listen again and repeat the proverbs with the same stress.*

SKILL PRESENTATION

Sentence stress is what gives English its rhythm or "beat." English-speakers stress the most important words in a sentence—they say those words a little more strongly.

Listening for sentence stress can help you understand English better. The stressed words are key words—the words that carry the most important meaning. If you are able to listen for those words, you can understand a lot, even if you don't understand every word.

We can divide words into two groups. **Content words** are the more important words in a sentence. They carry the most meaning and so receive more stress. **Function words** are short, less important words. They give the sentence its grammatical form but do not carry much meaning.

Here are some examples of content and function words.

Content Words (stressed)		Function Words (unstressed)	
Question words:	*what, where, how long*	Articles:	*a, an, the*
Nouns:	*man, Sam, teacher*	Pronouns:	*she, we, they*
Most verbs:	*eat, enjoy, turn on*	Prepositions:	*at, by, into*
Adjectives:	*big, soft, happy*	Conjunctions:	*and, but, because*
Adverbs:	*fast, never, loudly*	The verb *be*:	*am, is, were*
		Auxiliary verbs:	*are, does, can*

Note
Negative auxiliary verbs, such as *can't, don't, won't, haven't,* as well as negative words *not* and *no* are usually stressed.

☑ Check Yourself

A. *Practice with a partner. Are these content or function words? Write* C *for content or* F *for function.*

1. _____ jump
2. _____ are
3. _____ for
4. _____ sad
5. _____ play

6. _____ quick
7. _____ I
8. _____ didn't
9. _____ my
10. _____ because

11. _____ long
12. _____ John
13. _____ they
14. _____ isn't
15. _____ eat

16. _____ onto
17. _____ the
18. _____ will
19. _____ always
20. _____ why

B. 🎧 *Underline the content words in each sentence. Then listen. Pay attention to the way the speaker stresses the content words.*

1. I'd like a cup of soup and a large salad.
2. Some of my friends gave me a surprise party.
3. Jun was taking a test when his phone suddenly rang.
4. Where are you and your wife going on your honeymoon?
5. Did you and Tom get Rachael a present for her birthday?
6. I went to a great concert at the university on Saturday.

C. 🎧 *Listen again and repeat each sentence with the correct stress.*

PRACTICE

■ EXERCISE 1

A. *Work with a partner. Add function words to make a complete sentence. (More than one answer is possible.)*

1. Meg / can't / drive / lost / license *Meg can't drive because she lost her license* .
2. keys / bag / table _____.
3. parents / coming / weekend _____.
4. Brian / never / lived / abroad _____.
5. don't / have / enough / money / taxi _____.
6. usually / has / breakfast / nine o'clock _____.
7. like / tea / hate / coffee _____.
8. where / get / cool / jacket _____?

B. *Take turns saying your sentences from Exercise A. Stress the content words.*

■ EXERCISE 2

A. *Work with a partner. Add content words to make a complete sentence. (More than one answer is possible.)*

1. they / to / the _____*They went to the beach.*_____.
2. my / is / under / the _____.
3. you / should / him _____.
4. and / I / are _____.

(continued)

5. some / are / in / the _____.

6. the / is / next to / the _____.

7. she / is / but / she _____.

8. is / your _____.

B. *Take turns saying your sentences from Exercise A. Stress the content words.*

■ **EXERCISE 3**

A. 🎧 *Listen to each conversation and underline the stressed words.*

Conversation 1

A: <u>Aren't</u> you <u>ready</u>?

B: I found my coat, my hat, and my scarf but I can't find my gloves.

A: Did you look in the closet?

B: I looked in the closet, under my bed, and in my coat pockets. I think I lost them.

A: Well, you need some gloves. It's cold and windy outside.

B: I could borrow my sister's gloves. But where are they?

Conversation 2

A: What are you doing? Checking your email? Watching a video?

B: Oh, I'm looking for a cheap airfare.

A: To where?

B: To Chicago. My sister lives there. She's getting married in August.

A: That's great! Is she having a big wedding?

B: No, just family and some close friends. They want a small, quiet wedding.

Conversation 3

A: Can I help you?

B: I'm looking for a shirt, a dress shirt.

A: And what is your size?

B: Oh, it's not for me. It's for my brother. I think he's a medium.

A: Do you want long- or short-sleeved?

B: Long-sleeved, and silk if you have any.

A: We have some very nice silk shirts here. And we have some neckties too.

B. *Practice the conversations in Exercise A with a partner.*

■ EXERCISE 4

A. *Underline the words that should be stressed in each conversation.*

Conversation 1

Man: This <u>place</u> is <u>really</u> <u>nice</u>.

Woman: Yeah, I <u>love</u> the food here
And the service here is great.

Man: Do you know what you want?

Woman: I think so. I'm going to get
some soup and a sandwich.
And then some dessert.

Man: Wow! You're hungry!

Woman: Yes, I am. I'm starving! Where's our waitress?

Waitress: Here I am. Sorry to keep you waiting.

Conversation 2

Waitress: Are you ready to order?

Man: Yes, I'd like a seafood salad and a small bottle of water.

Woman: What's the soup today?

Waitress: Chicken and rice. It's very good.

Woman: OK. I'll have a bowl of soup and a tuna sandwich. And for dessert I'd like
the strawberry cheesecake.

Waitress: Anything to drink?

Woman: Can I get a large iced tea?

Waitress: With lemon?

Woman: Yes, thank you.

Conversation 3

Waiter: A large iced tea and a seafood salad for you.

Man: Um, the iced tea isn't mine. It's hers.

Woman: The water is his.

Waiter: And a cup of chicken and rice soup.

Woman: Um, I ordered a bowl of soup. And a tuna sandwich.

Waiter: You did?

Woman: Yes.

Waiter: I'm very sorry. I'll get it for you.

Man: Do you want some of my salad?

Woman: I'll wait. It's strange. The service here is usually very good.

B. 🎧 *Listen and check your answers to Exercise A. Then practice the conversations in groups of three.*

■ EXERCISE 5

A. 🎧 *Listen to four short conversations. Write only the content words.*

1.
A: *What doing?*
B: _____
A: _____?
B: _____. _____.

2.
A: _____ _____?
B: _____. _____
_____.
A: _____.
B: _____ _____
_____.

3.
A: _____ _____.
B: _____. _____.
A: _____?
B: _____. _____.

4.
A: _____?
B: _____ _____?
A: _____. _____
_____.
B: _____?

B. *Compare your answers to Exercise A with a partner. Then use the content words to write your own conversations. Present one of your conversations for the class.*

PUT IT TOGETHER

Quotations

Many people enjoy reading or collecting quotations—interesting sayings from famous or not-so-famous people. An interesting quotation can make you think about things in a new way. It can also give you insight into the life of the person who said it.

A. Vocabulary Preview *Study the words and their definitions. Then use the words to complete the sentences below.*

passionately	strongly; emotionally
curious	eager to know or learn
perseverance	continuing to try at something until you succeed
journey	a long trip
drive out	force someone or something to go away
pessimist	a person who thinks that whatever happens will be bad
optimist	a person who thinks that whatever happens will be good
interrupt	to cause someone to stop what they are doing

1. Please don't _____ me when I'm speaking. It isn't polite.

2. Tom is always ready for something bad to happen. He is such a _____.

3. The woman used a broom to _____ the mouse she found in the kitchen.

4. A cat is a _____ animal. Cats like to examine every new thing that they see.

5. Completing a marathon isn't easy. It takes a lot of hard work and _____.

6. The _____ to the top of the mountain will take several days.

7. I don't worry about bad things happening. I'm a real _____.

8. Many people in Brazil are_____ interested in soccer.

Remember

Content words (nouns, most verbs, adjectives, adverbs, and negative auxiliary verbs) usually receive sentence stress.
Function words (articles, pronouns, prepositions, conjunctions, the verb *to be* and affirmative auxiliary verbs) are usually unstressed.

B. *Read each quotation and underline the words that should be stressed.*

1. "I have no special talents. I am only passionately curious."
   Albert Einstein, German/Swiss/U.S. physicist (1879–1955)

2. "If we are to reach real peace in this world, we shall have to begin with the children."
   Mahatma Gandhi, Indian civil rights leader (1869–1948)

3. "A business that makes nothing but money is a poor business."
   Henry Ford, U.S. industrialist (1863–1947)

4. "Perseverance is failing nineteen times and succeeding the twentieth."
   Julie Andrews, British actor, singer and author (1935 -)

(continued)

5. "I am only one, but I am one. I cannot do everything, but I can do something. I must not fail to do the something that I can do."
Helen Keller, U.S. blind and deaf author and lecturer, (1880–1968)

6. "A journey of a thousand miles must begin with a single step."
Lao Tzu, Chinese philosopher (sixth century B.C.)

7. "Darkness cannot drive out darkness: only light can do that. Hate cannot drive out hate: only love can do that."
Martin Luther King, U.S. civil rights leader (1929–1968)

8. "If you have knowledge, let others light their candles in it."
Margaret Fuller, U.S. journalist and women's rights leader (1810–1850)

9. "Life is what happens while you are busy making other plans."
John Lennon, British musician and member of The Beatles (1940–1980)

10. "The pessimist sees the difficulty in every opportunity. The optimist sees the opportunity in every difficulty."
Winston Churchill, British prime minister (1874–1965)

11. "Never interrupt your enemy when he is making a mistake." *Napoleon Bonaparte, French ruler (1769–1821)*

12. "I am not young enough to know everything." *Oscar Wilde, British dramatist (1854–1900)*

C. 🎧 ***Listen to the quotations in Exercise B and check that you underlined the correct words. Then take turns reading the quotations with a partner.***

D. ***Work in small groups. Choose three quotations in Exercise B to discuss. Do you like the quotations? Do you agree with them? Why or why not?***

Folktale: How Bear Lost His Tail

Folktales are old, traditional stories. Folktales are a part of every culture around the world. In the past, people often created these stories to explain things that happened in nature. In this section, you will hear a folktale from Native American culture that explains why bears do not have tails.

■ EXERCISE 2

A. Vocabulary Preview *Match the words to their definitions. Use a dictionary if necessary.*

_____ 1. bushy a. not deep; not far from top to bottom

_____ 2. shiny b. broke suddenly into two parts

_____ 3. trick c. a clever plan meant to deceive or fool someone

_____ 4. shallow d. having thick hair or fur; full

_____ 5. paw e. reflecting light; bright

_____ 6. snoring f. held firmly, so that something cannot get away

_____ 7. trapped g. an animal's (a dog's, a cat's, a bear's) foot

_____ 8. snapped off h. breathing noisily when asleep

How Bear Lost His Tail

Part 1

In the old days, Bear had a tail. It was long and bushy and shiny, and Bear waved it around proudly so that the other animals could see it. Fox saw Bear do this and decided to trick him. As everyone knows, Fox was famous for his clever tricks.

It was winter, and snow covered the ground and ice covered the lake. Fox made a hole in the ice over the lake near a place where Bear often walked. When Bear came by, he saw that Fox had already caught several big fish and, as he watched, Fox pulled his red tail from the hole in the ice and there was another fat fish with the tip of Fox's tail in its mouth.

"Good afternoon, brother," Fox said.

"Good afternoon," Bear said. He looked hungrily at the fish. "Fox, can you teach me to fish like that?"

Part 2

"Certainly, brother," said Fox. "But you can't fish here—I've already caught all the fish in this part of the lake." Fox led Bear to a shallow part of the lake where he knew there were no fish and cut a hole in the ice. "Now just stand here with your back to the hole and slowly move your tail around and soon a fish will bite it. As soon as you feel the bite of the fish, pull your tail out of the water quickly and grab the fish with your paws."

E. 🎧 *Listen to Part 2. Notice the stressed words. Do they match the words you underlined?*

F. *Work with a partner. Read Part 3 of the folktale and underline the words that you think should be stressed.*

Part 3

Bear lay down with his tail in the icy water and waited for a fish to bite, but of course there were no fish there. Soon Bear fell asleep. Meanwhile, Fox went home and slept in his own bed. When he came back in the morning, Bear was snoring so loudly that the ice was shaking. "Good morning, brother!" said Fox.

Bear woke up and realized that Fox had tricked him. "I'll get you for this," Bear shouted and jumped at Fox. But the water in the hole had frozen during the night and Bear's beautiful tail was trapped in the ice. When he jumped at Fox, his tail snapped off! The quick Fox ran off laughing. And that is why, today, bears have only short tails, and they still don't trust foxes.

G. 🎧 *Listen to Part 3. Notice the stressed words. Do they match the words you underlined?*

■ EXERCISE 3

A. *Work in a group. Take turns reading aloud the folktale in Exercise 2. Remember to stress the content words.*

B. *Talk about folktales in your culture. Discuss the questions:*

1. What kinds of folktales are popular in your culture? What are the titles of some folktales that you know?

2. Are there any folktales with animal characters in them? What are they about?

3. Do you have a favorite folktale? What is it about?

PART

2

Comprehension Focus

Understanding Main Ideas and Details

Unit Warm Up

Work with a partner. Look at the picture. What kinds of things are the people listening to?

SKILL PRESENTATION

Listening for Main Ideas

When we listen, it's important to understand the general idea or topic of what we hear. This is listening for the main idea. When you listen for main ideas, don't try to understand every word or to catch the small details. Instead, listen only for the most important idea or the overall topic. Understanding the main idea of what you are listening to can then help you better understand the additional details.

☑ Check Yourself

A. 🎧 *Listen to the voicemail message. Check (✓) what the message is about.*

☐ a missed flight   ☐ a cancelled flight   ☐ an early flight

B. 🎧 *Listen and write the answers to the questions.*

1. Where is the speaker? _____

2. Who is the announcement for? _____

3. What is the purpose of the announcement? _____

C. 🎧 *Listen to the conversation. Circle the topics that the speakers discuss.*

weather   prices   transportation   hotels   sightseeing

Listening for Details

Details include specific pieces of information, such as names, numbers, dates, etc. Often the details of what we listen to can be very important. It can mean the difference between writing down a phone number correctly or incorrectly, getting on the right or wrong bus after you ask for bus information, or going to the right or wrong gate at the airport after you hear a gate change announcement.

☑ Check Yourself

A. 🎧 *Listen to the phone call. Circle the correct answers.*

1. The woman wants a room for (*one night / two nights*).

2. She books a (*single / double*) room.

3. The garden view room is (*$109 / $129*).

B. 🎧 *Listen and write the answers to the questions.*

1. What is the flight number? _____

2. Where is the flight going? _____

3. What gate will it leave from? _____

4. When will boarding begin? _____

C. 🎧 *Listen to the conversation. Check (✓) the things the man decides to pack.*

☐ a tent   ☐ a towel   ☐ a book   ☐ a radio

☐ a sleeping bag   ☐ toothpaste   ☐ a flashlight   ☐ food

☐ soap   ☐ a toothbrush   ☐ matches   ☐ water

PRACTICE

> **Tip**
> When you listen, you may want to take short notes on some of the things you hear, such as key words, numbers, and names. This can help you better understand the main ideas and any details.

■ EXERCISE 1

A. 🎧 **Main Idea** *Listen to Beth talk about a recent trip. Check (✓) the topics she talks about.*

☐ where she went   ☐ when she went

☐ who she traveled with   ☐ how long she stayed

☐ what she ate   ☐ what the weather was like

B. 🎧 **Details** *Listen again. Circle the correct answers.*

1. There were about (*1200 / 2200*) passengers on the cruise.
2. Beth went with (*her friend / her friend and parents*).
3. Beth (*likes / doesn't like*) to lie in the sun by the pool.
4. Beth says the food on the cruise was (*beautiful / amazing*).
5. It was (*sunny / sunny but sometimes rainy*).
6. Beth wouldn't go again because (*it was boring / she was seasick*).

■ EXERCISE 2

A. 🎧 **Main Idea** *Listen to a talk on unusual types of travel. Number the forms of travel from 1 to 4 in the order they are discussed. (There is one extra.)*

_____ space travel   _____ movie travel   _____ ghost travel

_____ dark travel   _____ star travel

B. 🎧 **Details** *Listen again and write the answers to the questions.*

1. If you're interested in movie travel, what should you be careful of?

_____

2. What kind of ghost tours do many cities have?

_____

3. What makes it difficult to see stars?

_____

4. Where did the idea of "dark sky parks" start?

_____

5. How much has space travel cost in the past?

_____

Volunteer Tourism

What kind of vacations do you enjoy? Can you imagine taking a vacation where you had to work hard every day—for example, working on a farm, teaching at a school, building houses—for no money? It's called volunteer tourism, and it's becoming a popular way to travel.

■ **EXERCISE 3**

A. Vocabulary Preview *Read each sentence. Then circle the best definition for the underlined word(s).*

1. I'm a <u>volunteer</u> at an animal shelter. I sometimes help out there after work.

    a. someone who works for no pay   b. someone who works part-time

2. I'd love to find a career that would <u>combine</u> working with children and traveling.

    a. support   b. mix

3. I worked for a month at a summer camp last year. I actually got <u>college credit</u> for it.

    a. payments to be used   b. unit of study received for successful
       for school or university   completion of a university course

4. Before you offer her the job, let's <u>evaluate</u> her computer skills.

    a. judge how good something is   b. give training in

5. We really value your <u>expertise</u>. We feel you'd be a great addition to our team.

    a. special skills and knowledge   b. positive job references

6. Never sign anything until you read the <u>fine print</u>.

    a. most important information   b. details, often in difficult-to-understand
                                          language

B. 🎧 *Listen to a presentation on volunteer tourism. Number the tips from 1 to 5 in the order they are presented. (There is one extra tip.)*

_____ Read everything.   _____ Evaluate the organizations.

_____ Decide on a program.   _____ Stay involved.

_____ Start your search.   _____ Think about your interests.

C. 🎧 *Listen again. Read the sentences and write* **T** *for true or* **F** *for false.*

_____ 1. Volunteer tourism is volunteering instead of taking a vacation.

_____ 2. You can do volunteer tourism abroad or at home.

_____ 3. All volunteer tourism programs involve working with the environment.

_____ 4. Most people start their search at a tourist office.

_____ 5. You can get college credit for a volunteer tourism program.

_____ 6. There are some volunteer tourism groups that don't charge any money.

_____ 7. It's a good idea to write to someone who has already done a trip.

D. *Correct any false statements in Exercise C. Then compare your answers with a partner.*

■ EXERCISE 4

A. *Work in a group. Discuss these examples of volunteer tourism programs. Which ones do you think would be the most interesting? Why?*

- building homes for families in need
- cleaning up a riverside or lake
- helping rescue abandoned or lost animals
- entertaining sick children at a hospital
- fixing hiking trails in a national park
- teaching or training people

B. *With your group, plan a volunteer tourism project in your neighborhood or city for overseas tourists. Think about the answers to these questions and take notes.*

1. What kinds of projects are you interested in?
2. What specifically needs to be done?
3. How many people will be on the project
4. How long will the project take?
5. Where will the volunteers stay?
6. What will you do about food?
7. How will you pay for the project?
8. What fun vacation activities will you plan?

C. *Present your volunteer tourism project from Exercise B to the class.*

Applying Your Skills For additional practice listening for main ideas and details, turn to Part 2, Unit 4, pages 80–84 and Unit 5, pages 85–90.

Making Inferences

Unit Warm Up

Work with a partner. Look at the pictures and discuss the questions.

- What do you think the people are saying?
- How do you think they are feeling? Why do you think so?
- How do you think the pair of people in each picture are related?

SKILL PRESENTATION

Making Inferences from Information We Hear

While we may understand all of what we hear, there is often other information that's not stated directly by the speaker. We often understand some information *indirectly* and have to make guesses about what we hear based on our knowledge of the situation. This is called making inferences, and we do this all the time when we listen. For example, you made inferences when you discussed the picture in the Unit Warm Up.

We can make inferences about people—their ages, relationships, feelings, attitudes, and opinions. We can also infer information about a situation, such as what is happening and what will happen next.

☑ Check Yourself

A. 🎧 *Listen to a woman describe what she did at her job last night. Check (✓) her job.*

☐ a nurse   ☐ a doctor   ☐ a police officer   ☐ a race car driver   ☐ a chef

B. 🎧 *Listen to four conversations. Write where each conversation is taking place.*

1. _____   3. _____

2. _____   4. _____

C. 🎧 *Listen to part of a job interview. Check (✓) the statements that are probably true.*

1. ☐ The man worked at Pathway Market as a teenager.

2. ☐ The man was a cashier at Pathway Market.

3. ☐ The man liked his job at Pathway Market.

4. ☐ The man had a different job in college.

5. ☐ The man didn't get good grades in college.

6. ☐ The man hasn't worked in a coffee shop before.

7. ☐ The woman is the owner of the coffee shop.

8. ☐ The woman will offer the man the job tomorrow.

Making Inferences from a Speaker's Tone of Voice

We can also make inferences based on *how* a speaker says something. A speaker's tone of voice can tell us how he or she really feels about something (even when the speaker's actual words may say something else). For example, we may infer that the speaker is happy, upset, confident, uncertain, or nervous.

🎧 *Listen to a boss talk to four of her employees. How do you think she feels in each conversation? Circle the correct answer.*

1. happy	angry	uncertain
2. confused	tired	stressed
3. embarrassed	bored	confident
4. nervous	pleased	upset

PRACTICE

■ EXERCISE 1

A. 🎧 *Listen to the clues to four riddles. What is each person's job? Write your guesses.*

1. _____   3. _____

2. _____   4. _____

B. *Compare your guesses to Exercise A with a partner.*

■ EXERCISE 2

A. Vocabulary Preview *Read each sentence. Then circle the best definition for the underlined word(s).*

1. I'm <u>delighted</u> to see you! I have a wonderful weekend planned for us.

   a. very nervous and worried   b. very pleased and happy

2. I have to meet with my <u>supervisor</u>. I hope she's happy with my work.

   a. someone who manages other people's work   b. someone who interviews you for a job

3. You should get your ticket <u>in advance</u>. That movie is extremely popular.

   a. at a discount   b. ahead of time

4. This cup of coffee is so full that I'm afraid that I'll <u>spill</u> it.

   a. to cause to run or flow from a container   b. to cause a serious burn

5. Do your parents <u>allow</u> you to stay out past midnight?

   a. to get angry at someone for something   b. to let someone do something

6. There's a lot of <u>security</u> at airports these days. But I guess that's a good thing.

   a. what's done to keep people safe   b. large groups of people

B. 🎧 **Details** *Listen to a boss discussing office rules. Then read the statements. Write* **T** *for true and* **F** *for false.*

_____ 1. If you are sick one day, you don't need a doctor's note.

_____ 2. If you are sick for two or more days, you need a doctor's note.

_____ 3. You must request a personal day two days in advance.

_____ 4. You can take your lunch break anytime between 11:30 and 1:30.

_____ 5. If you don't take a lunch break, you can go home early.

_____ 6. You aren't allowed to bring drinks to your desk.

_____ 7. You must turn off your computer at night.

_____ 8. Everyone will need a photo ID to enter the building.

C. 🎧 **Inference** *Listen again. Check (✓) the statements that are probably true.*

1. ☐ There are meetings at this company every week.

2. ☐ Some employees have used sick days as personal days in the past.

3. ☐ The employees will like the rule about personal days.

4. ☐ Most employees have been taking two-hour lunch breaks.

5. ☐ Some employees who didn't take lunch breaks went home early in the past.

6. ☐ Someone spilled coffee on his or her computer last week.

7. ☐ Most employees won't want to turn off their computers at night.

8. ☐ There will be better security in the building.

■ **EXERCISE 3**

A. 🎧 **Main Idea** *Listen to two people talking about the new office rules.* *Check (✓) the topics they discuss.*

☐ the new sick-day rule   ☐ the lunch-hour rule

☐ a surprise party   ☐ Mark's opinion about his new supervisor

☐ who spilled coffee on a computer   ☐ the new security rules

☐ their pictures on their photo IDs   ☐ where to go for lunch tomorrow

B. 🎧 **Inference** *Listen again. Circle the correct answer to each question.*

1. What is Allison and Mark's relationship?

   a. co-workers   b. boss and employee

2. How does Allison feel about bringing in a doctor's note if she's sick?

   a. She thinks it's reasonable.   b. She's annoyed.

3. Which new policy does Allison find confusing?

    a. the lunch-hour policy   b. the personal days policy

4. How does Mark feel about the manager's opinion about drinks at desks?

    a. He feels annoyed.   b. He agrees.

5. Why does Mark have a new computer?

    a. He spilled something on his old one.   b. He turned it off and it wouldn't start.

6. Where will Mark have lunch tomorrow?

    a. in a restaurant with Allison   b. at his desk

C. Work in groups. Discuss these questions.

1. What are some rules at your school or workplace? Do you agree with all of them?

2. What would you do if you disagreed with a new rule?

■ EXERCISE 4

Work in a group. Use your inferencing skills to try to solve these puzzles. The answers are at the bottom of the page.

Puzzle 1

A police officer spoke to five local thieves, trying to find out who stole a bicycle from outside a high school. Here are their statements. It was well known that each thief told exactly one lie. Who stole the bicycle?

    Alan: It wasn't Eddie. It was Brian.

    Brian: It wasn't Chuck. It wasn't Eddie.

    Chuck: It was Eddie. It wasn't Alan.

    David: It was Chuck. It was Brian.

    Eddie: It was David. It wasn't Alan.

Puzzle 2

Four women competed in a race. Susan Brown beat Megan. Miss Parker beat Lynne. Anne was not third. Miss Jones was not last. Miss Smith, who was not Anne, came just after Susan. Which girl was first, second, third, and fourth?

> **Applying Your Skills** For additional practice making inferences, turn to Part 2, Unit 5, pages 85–90 and Unit 6, pages 91–95.

Answers

Puzzle 1: The thief is Chuck.

Puzzle 2: (1) Anne Parker   (2) Lynne Jones   (3) Susan Brown   (4) Megan Smith

Unit Warm Up

Work with a partner. Look at the picture. Describe what happens when the man slips on ice. Use these verbs to help you.

bite   drop   fall   kick   move   pull   push   release   slip   walk

SKILL PRESENTATION

Sequence Signal Words

When we listen, we often need to understand the sequence of steps or events. For example, this skill is important when we listen to directions to a place, instructions for how to do something, or a series of events that make up a story. If we don't follow the sequence, we may get lost, miss a necessary step in the instructions, or not fully understand a good story. Often the speaker will help you follow the sequence by using signal words and phrases.

Example

First, *insert your card into the ATM.*

Next, *enter your personal identification number.*

Then, *press OK.*

After that, *remove your cash.*

Finally, *take your card and receipt.*

The words *before* and *after* also commonly indicate order in a sequence.

Example

> *I brush my teeth* **before** *I go to bed.*
>
> *I go to bed* **after** *I brush my teeth.*

Other words or expressions can also indicate sequence:

- *once* = after
- *as* = at the same time
- *as soon as* = immediately after
- *until* = up to that time

Example

> **Once** *I have a cup of coffee, I begin to feel awake.*
>
> *I always wake up* **as** *the sun comes up.*
>
> *I take a shower* **as soon as** *I get out of bed.*
>
> *I don't leave the house* **until** *I check my email.*

☑ Check Yourself

A. 🎧 **Listen to the recipe. Then circle the correct sequence signal words to complete the sentences below.**

No Bake Chocolate Peanut Butter Cookies

Ingredients

2 cups sugar	Mix the sugar and cocoa in a pot.
1/2 cup cocoa	Add the milk and butter.
1/2 cup milk	Cook until the mixture starts to boil.
1/2 cup butter	Stir in the peanut butter and boil for one minute.
1/4 cup peanut butter	Remove from heat and stir in the oats and chips.
3 cups oats	Drop by the spoonful onto a cookie sheet.
1/4 cup chocolate chips	Let cool for ten minutes. Enjoy!

1. (*Before* / *After*) you add the milk and butter, mix the sugar and cocoa in a pot.

2. (*Once* / *Until*) you add the milk and butter, cook the mixture.

3. Don't stir in the peanut butter (*once* / *until*) the mixture starts to boil.

4. (*Before* / *As soon as*) you remove the mixture from the heat, add the oats and chips.

5. Try a cookie (*as* / *after*) ten minutes.

B. 🎧 *Listen to a woman talk about her typical Saturday. Write what she does at each of these times.*

9:00	Noon	1:30	4:00	7:30

C. 🎧 *Listen to a news report about a stolen car. Number the events in order from 1 to 8.*

_____ Ed arrested the thief.

_____ The thief went to the supermarket parking lot.

_____ Alice reported her car as stolen.

_____ Ed called Alice's phone.

__1__ Alice parked her car in front of the post office.

_____ Someone stole Alice's car.

_____ Ed said he wanted to buy Alice's car.

_____ Alice forgot to take her cell phone with her.

Understanding Processes

Another common type of sequence describes the steps in a process. The process may describe how something is made (for example, candy bars), how something is formed (for example, a tornado), or how something is done (for example, a magic trick).

When we explain processes in English, we often use the passive voice. The passive voice is formed by using the verb *be* plus the past participle of the main verb.

Example

A tornado is formed when cold air meets warm air.

When they are ripe, the coffee beans are picked by hand.

☑ Check Yourself

A. 🎧 *Listen to an explanation of how a perfect cup of British tea is made. Use the correct sequence signal words to complete the sentences.*

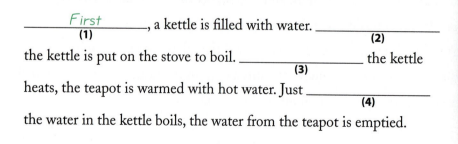

_____*First*_____, a kettle is filled with water. _____
    (1)   **(2)**

the kettle is put on the stove to boil. _____ the kettle
                                    (3)

heats, the teapot is warmed with hot water. Just _____
                                           (4)

the water in the kettle boils, the water from the teapot is emptied.

_____, loose tea is placed in the bottom of the teapot.
(5)

_____, the boiling water is poured over the tea.
(6)

_____ _____ _____ the water is poured, the teapot is covered.
(7)

_____, the tea sits for a few minutes. _____, the tea is poured
(8)   (9)

into cups. Milk and sugar are _____ added, if desired.
(10)

B. 🎧 *Listen to a talk on how hailstones are formed. Check (✓) the true information.*

1. ☐ Hailstones are balls of ice with a regular shape.

2. ☐ Hailstones begin as very small drops of water in a cloud.

3. ☐ After they begin to fall, they're pushed up by strong winds.

4. ☐ Once the water drops reach the cool air, they are frozen.

5. ☐ As the frozen drops fall again, they begin to get smaller.

6. ☐ As soon as a hailstone is frozen, it falls on the ground.

7. ☐ The most common size hailstones are the size of a golf ball.

PRACTICE

■ EXERCISE 1

Bethany's Story

Bethany Hamilton is a young surfer from Hawaii. You will learn about her amazing story.

> **Tip**
> When you listen to a sequence of events in someone's life, listen for time expressions such as times, days of the week, months, and years.

A. 🎧 **Details** *Listen to a talk about Bethany Hamilton. Circle the answers.*

1. How old was Bethany when she entered her first surfing contest?

    a. seven

    b. eight

    c. nine

2. How many people were surfing with Bethany when the shark bit her?

    a. one

    b. two

    c. three

3. How long was Bethany in the hospital?

    a. almost a week

    b. more than two weeks

    c. less than a month

4. What happened in 2004?

    a. Bethany wrote a book.

    b. Bethany won a surfing contest.

    c. Bethany started a business.

5. What's the name of the documentary film about Bethany's life?

    a. *Follow Your Dreams*

    b. *Soul Surfer*

    c. *Heart of a Soul Surfer*

6. What kind of business did Bethany start?

    a. a perfume business

    b. a surfboard company

    c. a surfing school

B. 🎧 **Sequence** *Listen again. Number the events in order from 1 to 9.*

_____ She won her first surfing contest.

_____ She entered the perfume business.

_____ She learned how to surf with one arm.

_____ Her book was made into a movie.

_____ A shark bit her arm off.

_____ She won her first national title.

_____ She wrote a book about her experience.

_____ A documentary film was made about her.

1 Her parents taught her how to surf.

C. *Discuss the questions with the class.*

    • What qualities do you think Bethany possesses?

    • Do you know anyone else who has these qualities?

Making Olive Oil

Even if you don't use olive oil for cooking, chances are you've eaten food cooked with olive oil. But do you know how olive oil is made? You will learn about this interesting process.

A. **Vocabulary Preview** *Read the sentences. Then write each underlined verb next to its definition below.*

- You should <u>shake</u> this bottle of salad dressing before you use it.
- Please cut off the tops of those carrots and <u>discard</u> them.
- My two-year-old son loves to <u>spin</u> in circles until he falls down.
- Some animals <u>store</u> food for use during the winter.
- Please <u>press</u> firmly when you sign these documents.
- I like to <u>grind</u> my own coffee beans. It really brings out the flavor.
- The farmers usually <u>harvest</u> the corn in September or October.
- I'm going to <u>gather</u> some wood and build a small campfire.

1. _____ bring in a crop for use or sale
2. ____*shake*____ move up and down or side to side quickly
3. _____ bring things together to the same place
4. _____ put something away for use in the future
5. _____ throw something away
6. _____ crush something into smaller pieces
7. _____ push something against a surface
8. _____ turn around and around quickly

Remember

When describing processes, the speaker often uses the passive voice. Listen carefully for the past participles of verbs as well as sequence signal words to follow the sequence.

B. *Write the past participle for each verb. Then compare with a partner.*

1. shake ____*shaken*____
2. discard _____
3. spin _____
4. store _____
5. press _____
6. grind _____
7. harvest _____
8. gather _____

C. 🎧 **Details** *Listen to a talk on the process of making olive oil. Answer the questions.*

1. What is olive oil mainly used for today? _____
2. What's the best weather for growing olive trees? _____

3. What three countries make and sell the most olive oil?_____

4. When are olives harvested? _____

5. In the past, how were olives removed from trees? _____

6. Where is olive oil stored until it's shipped? _____

7. What color is the olive oil in clear glass bottles? _____

8. What happens to the flavor when the color changes? _____

D. 🎧 **Sequence** *Listen again. Use past participles to complete these steps in how to make olive oil.*

1. The olives are _____*removed*_____ from the trees.

2. The olives are _____ according to size, color, and quality.

3. Any bad olives are _____.

4. The olives are _____ for about a day.

5. The olives are _____ to the olive crusher.

6. The olives are _____ into a paste.

7. Water is _____ to the paste.

8. The paste is _____ for 20 to 30 minutes.

9. The paste is _____ under high pressure.

10. The paste is _____ to remove the water.

11. The oil is stored until it's ready to be _____.

12. Finally, the oil is canned or _____.

■ EXERCISE 3

A. *Prepare a two-minute talk about one of the following topics. Think about the sequence of events.*

- how to make your favorite dish
- instructions for how to do something
- a biography of someone
- directions from your home to another place
- something interesting that happened to you
- how something is made, formed, or done

B. *Work in a group. Take turns giving your talks. Answer any questions.*

Applying Your Skills For additional practice listening for sequence, turn to Part 2, Unit 5, pages 85–90 and Unit 6, pages 91–95.

The Problem with Eyewitnesses

Unit Warm Up

In this unit, you will listen to a talk about people who witness (see) a crime.

Work with a partner. Discuss the questions.

- Do you think you can usually believe what an eyewitness says? Why or why not?

- Look carefully at the picture for ten seconds. Then close your book and describe as many details as you can. Afterwards, check the picture again. What details did you remember? What did you miss?

LISTENING TASK

Before You Listen

A. Vocabulary Preview *Match the words to their definitions. Use a dictionary if necessary. Then use the words to complete the sentences below.*

_____ 1. intruder

_____ 2. wastebasket

_____ 3. take part in

_____ 4. throw away

_____ 5. versions

_____ 6. disguise

_____ 7. success rate

_____ 8. observant

a. able to notice things quickly and easily

b. a small container for trash

c. something (such as a mask or a wig) that is worn to hide one's identity

d. get rid of something one no longer wants or needs

e. participate; join in

f. slightly different forms of the same thing

g. the rate or percentage of accomplishing goals or achieving something

h. someone who comes into a place uninvited

11. I didn't recognize Andrew because he was wearing a _____.

12. Sandra doesn't _____ any sports at school. She doesn't enjoy exercise.

13. The police questioned a woman who had been an _____ to the bank robbery, but she couldn't describe the robber very well.

14. We thought we heard an _____ upstairs, but it was just the cat.

15. Don't put those cans in the _____. Recycle them instead.

16. I'm not very _____. I didn't notice that Johan had shaved his beard.

17. Marcos didn't know about the party _____. You should have seen his face when he walked into the room and everyone shouted, "Surprise!"

18. The police detective solved half her cases. She had a _____ of 50 percent.

19. Please don't _____ those documents—they're very important.

20. There are many _____ of this story, each one a little different.

B. Predict *The title of this unit is "The Problem with Eyewitnesses." Talk with the class. What do you think the "problems" are? What information do you think will be included in the talk?*

While You Listen

First Listening

🎧 **Sequence** *Listen to a speaker describe several experiments. Number the steps in order from 1 to 8.*

_____ The teacher returns to the classroom.

_____ The intruder moves the teacher's briefcase to the floor.

_____ The teacher comes into the classroom and places his briefcase on the desk.

_____ The intruder throws a piece of paper in the wastebasket.

_____ The students examine the photos.

_____ The intruder enters the classroom.

_____ The teacher asks the students if an intruder entered the classroom.

_____ The intruder changes the time on the clock.

Second Listening

A. 🎧 **Details** *Listen again. Then work with a partner. Use words or phrases from the box to complete the sentences.*

briefcase	experiments	make mistakes
changes	forty-five	observant
dark glasses	hat	photographs
disguise	identify	taking part
eyewitness	improve	twenty-five

1. Many people think that the easiest way to solve a mystery is to talk to an

   _____.

2. However, eyewitnesses sometimes _____.

3. Many _____ show that people have problems remembering things they have just seen.

4. In one experiment, an "intruder" comes into the room and moves the teacher's

   _____ to the floor.

5. She also _____ the time on the clock.

6. The intruder is really _____ in the experiment.

7. Then the students look at twenty _____ of the intruder.

8. Only about _____ percent of the students can identify the intruder.

9. About _____ percent of the students remember that she threw away a piece of paper.

10. In one version of this experiment, the intruder is wearing _____ and has a _____ pulled down over her forehead.

11. About the same percentage of students were able to identify the intruder even though she is wearing a _____.

12. The teacher tells the students that someone is going to take his briefcase and that they will have to _____ this person, but this does not _____ the students' success rate by very much.

13. The speaker says that everyone should be more _____.

B. 🎧 **Inference** *Listen to some short parts of the talk. Check (✓) the statements that are probably true.*

1. ☐ The speaker believes that eyewitnesses are the best way to solve crimes.

2. ☐ The speaker is surprised that such a small percentage of students could recognize the photograph of the intruder.

3. ☐ More students remember an unusual action than an ordinary action.

4. ☐ If a person wears a disguise, people will be less likely to recognize him or her later.

5. ☐ It's important to question eyewitnesses as soon as possible after an event.

6. ☐ The speaker thinks it is surprising that knowing about a memory test in advance does not improve the success rate by very much.

7. ☐ The speaker believes that his listeners can learn from the results of these experiences.

After You Listen

■ EXERCISE 1

Work with a partner. Discuss these questions. Then share your answers with the class.

1. The person who came into the classroom did three things. Which of these actions did most of the students remember? Why do you think they remembered this?

2. Why do you think eyewitnesses have problems identifying people they have seen?

3. Do you find it easy or difficult to remember people's faces? What features do you usually remember about people?

Test your memory. Work in groups of four. Follow these instructions:

- Each group member chooses three personal items and puts them on a desk or table where the group can see them.

- Arrange the items in three rows like this:

  X   X   X   X

  X   X   X   X

  X   X   X   X

- All group members look at the items for one minute and try to remember them in order.

- Write as many items as you can in order in the chart. Then compare your chart with your group members. Who remembered the most items?

1.	2.	3.	4.
5.	6.	7.	8.
9.	10.	11.	12.

The Whale's Tale

Unit Warm Up

In this unit, you will listen to an amazing true story about a whale.

Work with a partner. Discuss the questions.

- What do you know about whales?
- What do you see in the picture?
- What do you think is happening?

LISTENING TASK

Before You Listen

A. Vocabulary Preview *Match the words to their definitions. Use a dictionary if necessary. Then use the words to complete the sentences below.*

_____ **1.** rescue

_____ **2.** crab

_____ **3.** trap

_____ **4.** expert

_____ **5.** tangled

_____ **6.** wrap

_____ **7.** slap

_____ **8.** nudge

_____ **9.** wink

_____ **10.** immediately

a. tied or twisted together

b. a sea animal with a flat, round, shell-covered body and powerful claws

c. to push against lightly

d. to save or set free from danger or harm

e. without delay; at once; right away

f. a person with specialized skills or knowledge

g. a quick hit with the flat part of the hand or some other part of the body

h. to signal by closing and opening one eye quickly

i. to hold firmly, with little possibility of escape

j. to cover with cloth, paper, cords, or something similar

11. There was a mouse in the kitchen. The cat managed to _____ it, but somehow it escaped.

12. Be careful where you step. I saw a _____ go under the sand over there.

13. The cat was up at the very top of the tree. My neighbor climbed up there to _____ her.

14. After I finished high school, I didn't go to university _____. First I spent a year travelling and working at part-time jobs.

15. Jim knows a lot about whales and dolphins. He is an _____ on sea animals.

16. My headphone cord is always getting _____. It's annoying!

17. The mother gave the child a little _____ on the hand to stop him from touching the hot stove.

18. My friend Ernst was giving a speech. I think I saw him _____ at me to let me know that he saw me in the audience.

19. Rafael was almost falling asleep at the concert, so I decided to _____ him to wake him up.

20. I bought a gift for Ari's birthday, but I didn't have time to _____ it.

While You Listen

First Listening

A. 🎧 **Sequence** *Listen to the talk. Number the events in order from 1 to 10.*

_____ The whale is seen by some fishermen.

_____ The whale swims near the divers and "thanks" them.

_____ The whale swims in circles.

_____ The fishermen call an environmental group.

_____ The rescuers cut the ropes trapping the whale.

_____ The divers talk to a reporter.

_____ The team decides that they must get into the water.

_1_ The whale gets tangled in some ropes attached to crab traps.

_____ A rescue team arrives.

_____ The whale swims away.

B. Main Idea *Check (✓) the statement that best describes the main idea of the talk.*

☐ Divers often have to enter very cold water to rescue whales.

☐ Ropes used by crab fishermen are dangerous to whales and other sea life.

☐ A female whale was rescued by divers when it became tangled in fishing ropes.

☐ To express thanks, a female whale swam up and touched the divers who rescued it.

Second Listening

🎧 **Details** *Work in pairs. One student is A and one is B. Follow these instructions:*

- Read your own sentences. Think about what information might be missing.

- Listen to the talk again and complete your sentences. You will use the completed sentences to complete the next exercise.

Student A

1. This is a _____ story about a whale and the people who rescued her.

2. It happened about _____ miles from _____, California.

3. Some _____ saw the whale. It was not _____.

4. They used their _____ to call an environmental group.

5. A few hours later, a rescue team of _____ and whale _____ arrived to help.

(continued)

6. The ropes were wrapped around her _____ and her _____ and a rope was caught in her mouth.

7. They had to get in the cold water and cut the ropes with _____.

8. The whale could kill a diver with one _____ of her _____.

9. The whale didn't _____ away _____.

10. The divers thought that the whale was _____ them.

11. One diver told a _____ that he thought the whale _____ him and then winked at him.

12. That _____ said that it had been the greatest _____ of his whole life.

Student B

1. This is a true story about a _____ and the people who _____ her.

2. It happened in December, _____ in the _____ about 50 miles from San Francisco.

3. The whale was trapped in _____ attached to _____.

4. The fishermen used their radio to call an _____.

5. The group sent a rescue team of _____ and whale experts to help the whale.

6. The _____ were wrapped around her body and her tail and a rope was caught in her _____.

7. _____ the whale from the ropes was very _____ work.

8. The divers worked for several _____, and while they were working, the whale stayed _____.

9. It swam in _____ around the divers.

10. The whale came back and gently _____ the divers.

11. One diver said that he thought the whale nudged him and then _____ at him.

12. All of the divers said that it had been an experience that they would never _____.

AFTER YOU LISTEN

■ **EXERCISE 1**

Stay with your partner from Second Listening. Use your completed sentences to help you answer these questions.

1. When and where did this event happen?

   _____

2. Who first saw that the whale was in trouble?

   _____

3. What was the problem?

   _____

4. Who did the fishermen call?

   _____

5. Who came to help the whale?

   _____

6. What did the rescuers do?

   _____

7. Why was it a dangerous job?

   _____

8. What did the whale do after it was rescued?

   _____

9. Who did the divers talk to afterwards?

   _____

10. How did the divers feel?

   _____

Work in groups. Discuss these questions.

1. Why do you think the divers thought this was an important experience?

2. Do you think that the whale was really thanking the rescuers? Why or why not?

3. Do you know of any similar stories of animal rescues?

4. What are some other ways human activities such as fishing can be dangerous to ocean life?

5. Describe an unforgettable experience from your own life.

Art in the Fields

Unit Warm Up

In this unit, you will hear a longer talk about some very interesting works of art.

Work with a partner. Discuss the questions.

- What do you see in the picture?
- Where do you think this photograph was taken?
- How do you think the images were made?
- What kind of plants do you think are growing in the field?

LISTENING TASK

Before You Listen

Vocabulary Preview *Read the sentences. Then write each underlined word next to its definition below.*

- I didn't really <u>appreciate</u> that painting until I read about the artist.
- They built a new office building downtown. It's 80 <u>stories</u> tall.
- Jean-Paul does not like living in a big city. He'd rather live in a <u>rural</u> area.
- Some of the world's great <u>masterpieces</u> can be seen at the Louvre Museum in Paris.
- The first plan you showed me was simple, but this one is more <u>complex</u>.
- The measurements for the ingredients must be <u>precise</u> or the recipe won't work.
- That 3-D movie that I saw last night was incredible. I've never seen such an <u>extraordinary</u> film.
- I don't like the color of this tan sweater. I'm going to buy some green <u>dye</u>.

1. _____ countryside; away from the city
2. _____ recognize and enjoy the good qualities of something
3. _____ floors of a building
4. _____ great works of art
5. _____ a chemical used to change the color of something
6. _____ very special, unusual
7. _____ accurate; exact
8. _____ complicated; difficult

While You Listen

First Listening

A. 🎧 **Sequence** *Listen to the first part of a talk about the rice field patterns in Inakadate, Japan. Match each action with the time of year when it happens.*

_____ 1. late April   a. The rice is harvested.

_____ 2. summer   b. The patterns begin to appear in the fields.

_____ 3. September   c. The greatest number of visitors arrive.

_____ 4. October 4th   d. The farmers meet and plan their next works of art.

_____ 5. late fall   e. Farmers and volunteers plant the rice.

B. 🎧 **Sequence** *Listen to the second half of the talk. Match each year with the correct action.*

_____ 1. The works of art became more complicated.

_____ 2. More than 150,000 visitors came to see the art.

_____ 3. Farmers began creating art in their rice fields.

_____ 4. Computers were first used to plan the works of art.

_____ 5. Farmers signed an agreement that allowed them to make bigger works of art.

a. 1993

b. 2002

c. 2003

d. 2005

e. 2010

Second Listening

A. 🎧 **Main Idea and Details** *Listen and circle the best answer to complete each sentence.*

1. The images in the rice field are created by _____.

   a. planting rice with leaves of different colors

   b. using dyes to change the color of the water

   c. painting the leaves after they have grown

2. Most of the work on the art in the rice fields is done by _____.

   a. farmers and volunteers

   b. artists and tourists

   c. computer experts and farmers

3. Most tourists view the art by _____.

   a. walking through the rice fields

   b. going to the top of a nearby tower

   c. flying over the fields in a plane or helicopter

4. Farmers decide on the subject for next year's images _____.

   a. right after the rice is harvested

   b. when this year's art is at its peak

   c. just before they plant the rice

5. The original purpose of the art in Inakadate was to _____.

   a. help the local economy by bringing in tourists

   b. celebrate an important Japanese holiday

   c. compete with other towns that were creating rice-field art

(continued)

6. In 2005, Japanese farmers signed an agreement to _____.

    a. create art in fields belonging to more than one farmer

    b. always harvest rice on October 4

    c. equally divide the money that was collected from tourists

7. The speaker mentions the geoglyphs in ancient Peru because _____.

    a. like the rice field art, they can only be appreciated when viewed from above

    b. they are much more complicated than the rice field art of Japan

    c. unlike the rice field art, they were made in a desert

8. The main point of this whole talk is to _____.

    a. compare the rice-field art of Japan with the art of ancient Peru

    b. describe the process and the history of making rice-field art in Japan

    c. show how an ancient form of Japanese art was updated by technology

B. 🎧 **Inference** *You will hear some short comments about rice-field art. Listen and check (✓) True or False.*

	True	False
1. The photographs of the rice-field art are actually made by computers.	☐	☐
2. People in other parts of Japan want to attract tourists with rice-field art.	☐	☐
3. Viewing the rice-field art from a helicopter is very expensive.	☐	☐
4. The tower near the rice fields of Japan is seven stories high.	☐	☐
5. This scientist has proven that the Nazca used hot-air balloons.	☐	☐
6. People who created geoglyphs in Britain were influenced by the Nazca.	☐	☐
7. Some people may like the rice-field art because it is "temporary"—it does not last for a long time.	☐	☐

AFTER YOU LISTEN

■ EXERCISE 1

Work in groups. Discuss these questions.

- What do you think makes rice-field art so interesting to tourists?
- Would you pay money to see this kind of art?
- What are some other examples of art created from nature?

■ EXERCISE 2

A. *Work with a partner. Match the names of these extraordinary sights around the world to the countries where they are located.*

_____ 1. The Great Pyramid of Giza   a. China

_____ 2. The Great Wall   b. Egypt

_____ 3. The Taj Mahal   c. Italy

_____ 4. The Colosseum   d. Peru

_____ 5. Machu Picchu   e. India

B. *Join another pair. Compare your answers. Then discuss these questions.*

- What do you know about each place in Exercise A?
- Which places would you most like to visit? Why?

PART

3

Note-Taking Skills

Unit Warm Up

Look at the picture and listen to the conversation. Then discuss the questions in a group.

- Where are the people?
- What happened?
- Has this ever happened to you?

SKILL PRESENTATION

One of the most important skills for a student is taking clear notes. It's true that we remember more and learn better when we write things down. In fact, studies have shown that if we *don't* take notes during a talk, we may forget half of the information within twenty-four hours!

Reasons why taking notes is important:

- Taking notes helps you focus and keep your attention.
- Doing something active while you listen helps you remember and learn more.
- It helps you understand the most important ideas.
- It helps you know what information may be on an exam.
- It's a useful skill required for many jobs.

The exercises in this unit will help you learn how to take short, clear notes. The average speaker may speak anywhere from 125 to 140 words per minute, but an effective note-taker writes only about 25 words per minute. One of the first steps to developing good note-taking skills is learning to write short notes, not full sentences.

Content Words vs. Function Words

Remember that content words carry the important meaning of a sentence (see Part 1, Unit 5). Function words are the less important words and do not give a sentence much meaning. When taking notes, you don't usually need to write function words. Examples of function words include:

The verb *be*	am / is / were
Articles	a / an / the
Demonstratives	this / that / these

Auxiliary verbs	be / can / do / have
Pronouns	she / we / they
Some prepositions	at / from / of

In addition to function words, you should omit any information that isn't important.

☑ Check Yourself

Read the two sets of notes from the same talk about online user names. On Student A's notes, cross out the information that Student B omitted.

Student A

A recent online survey asked ~~people to answer the question~~ "What does your user name say about you?" ~~The results may surprise you.~~ 30% of the people in the survey said it's based on their actual name. 15% of the people said they just made it up. 7% answered that it's a word they like. 4% said it's just a random word they chose. 3% said it's from an animal and 1% said it's from a favorite celebrity. But the largest percentage, 40%, chose the answer "something else." Let's explore some of these other answers people chose...

Student B

Online survey asked "What does your user name say about you?" Results:

30% - based on actual name	3% - animal
15% - made up	1% - favorite celebrity
7% - word they like	largest percentage (40%) - something else
4% - random word	

Other answers:

PRACTICE

■ EXERCISE 1

Look at these sentences from a talk about personality and colors. Cross out any words that could be omitted in the notes. Then compare your answers with a partner.

1. Personality ~~is~~ patterns ~~of~~ thought, feelings, ~~and~~ behaviors.
2. It makes a person unique.
3. There are many personality tests that are available.
4. You can find them in magazines, books, and online.
5. Many people take these tests just for fun.
6. Some are based on scientific research, but many are not.
7. One example is a personality test about your favorite color.
8. The test shows that people with the same color preferences have similar personalities.

■ EXERCISE 2

A. *Read this section from the same talk and underline the most important information. Then compare your answers with a partner.*

Now let's look at <u>what</u> your <u>favorite color says about</u> your <u>personality</u>. If you <u>like black</u>, it means that you are <u>good with numbers</u> and <u>details</u>. If you like blue, you are very neat, but you don't trust other people very much. If you prefer green, you want to help others and are a good listener. If you love orange, you enjoy sports and the outdoors. If you like pink, you look for the good in people and want to make others happy. If purple is your favorite color, you want to learn and are always trying to improve yourself. Like red? Then you enjoy power and are good at making money. If you like yellow, you are careful but also good at making decisions. Finally, if you love white, then you appear to be shy, but in fact are not.

B. **Use the underlined information in Exercise A to complete these notes.**

What favorite color says about personality:
like black - good with numbers, details
blue - very neat, don't trust others
green -

LISTENING TASK

Birth order means whether you are a first, middle, last child, or an only child. In this Listening Task, you will hear a talk about how your birth order may be related to your personality.

Before You Listen

A. Topic Preview *Work in groups. Discuss these questions.*

- Do you have any brothers or sisters? If so, how many?

- Are you the oldest, youngest, or a middle child? Or are you an only child?

- How are the personalities of the children in your family similar or different?

B. Vocabulary Preview *Work with a partner. Check (✓) any words you already know. What do they mean? Look up any words you don't know. Then circle the correct word to complete each sentence.*

☐ ambitious ☐ diplomatic ☐ inflexible ☐ rebellious

☐ competitive ☐ immature ☐ outgoing ☐ responsible

☐ confident ☐ independent ☐ persuasive ☐ selfish

1. I'm very *(ambitious / outgoing)*. I try hard to be successful in life.

2. People say I'm *(independent / persuasive)*. I can easily get people to agree with me.

3. I can be *(diplomatic / inflexible)* at times. If I think I'm right, I rarely change my mind.

4. I'm *(rebellious / ambitious)*. I sometimes don't do what my parents tell me to.

5. I know I'm *(competitive / immature)*. I try to do things better than others.

6. I'm pretty *(selfish / independent)*. I don't need a lot of help from other people.

7. Some people say I'm *(immature / confident)* because I act younger than my age.

8. I'm pretty *(competitive / outgoing)*. I'm comfortable and friendly in social situations.

9. My parents trust me because I'm a *(persuasive / responsible)* person.

10. I'm very *(inflexible / diplomatic)*. I'm good at dealing with other people.

11. People think I'm a little *(responsible / selfish)* because I don't like to share.

12. I'm very *(confident / rebellious)*. I'm certain that I will be successful in my life.

C. 🎧 *Listen to the introduction from a talk about birth order and personality.*
   Complete the notes.

some researchers: order of birth affects personality:

- influences type of _____ you are

- connected to how you see _____ , _____ in school, and
  _____ you choose

Not everyone _____ - idea still _____ in popular culture

What _____ typical for different birth orders?

D. **Predict** *Check your notes with your teacher. What other information do you think will be*
   included in the talk?

While You Listen

First Listening

A. 🎧 **Guided Practice** *Listen to the first half of the talk and write the missing words.*

Traits of first-borns

want everything _____

get attention - never _____ enough

responsible, follow _____

ambitious, confident, get _____ grades

selfish - don't like to _____ things

choose _____ - high level of education

Traits of middle-borns

Competitive: have to compete with
first-borns, _____

Diplomatic - between two _____

Outgoing, rebellious, don't follow
_____

Choose _____ jobs (_____,
salespeople)

B. 🎧 **On Your Own** *Listen to the second half of the talk and take notes on a separate piece of paper. Start your notes like this. Remember to omit any unnecessary words.*

Personality traits of last-borns	Personality traits of only children

C. **Work with a partner. Compare your notes from Exercises A and B.**

Second Listening

🎧 **Check Your Notes** *Listen and check your notes from the First Listening. Add any information you missed or change any incorrect information. Then check your answers with your teacher.*

After You Listen

■ EXERCISE 1

A. **Work with a partner. Look back at your notes. What positive or negative adjectives describe each group of people? Complete the chart.**

	Positive	Negative
First-born		
Middle-born		
Last-born		
Only Children		

B. **Compare your chart with another pair. Did you agree on the positive and negative traits?**

■ EXERCISE 2

Work in a group. Discuss these questions.

- Do you agree with the description of your personality? Why or why not?
- Do you think you are more like another birth order's personality? Which one?
- Think about other people you know. Do the descriptions match their personalities?
- Do you think that the order of your birth affects personality?
- What, if anything, do you think the following can tell about your personality?

your name	your blood type	your favorite color
your month of birth	your year of birth	your handwriting

Using Abbreviations

Unit Warm Up

Read the email and look at the underlined abbreviations. Do you know what they mean? Compare your ideas with a partner.

Compose: e-mail message ⬓☐✕

To: Sarah

Subject: Pls. read ASAP!

Hi Sarah,

How are you? I couldn't wait to tell you the great news. I got a new job. I start on Sept. 1st. It's a job in the sales dept. of a computer store. I think it'll be really interesting. The store sells all kinds of cool electronics—cameras, software, games, etc. The schedule is great—I work Mon.–Thurs., so I have Fri.–Sun. off. My boss—the sales mgr.—is a really nice woman, too. I think I'm going to like working there!

How are things with you?

Love,
Jill

SKILL PRESENTATION

Abbreviations are all around us. We see them on signs, in newspapers, on websites, in emails, and in text messages. They're very useful for note-taking because they save writing time by representing longer words with short groups of letters. Look at the following types of abbreviations.

Standard Abbreviations

w/	with	**e.g./ex.**	for example
w/o	without	**i.e.**	in other words
b/c	because	**vs.**	versus
b/4	before	**etc.**	et cetera / and so on

Initials

EU	European Union		**S and D**	supply and demand
UN	Usnited Nations		**R and D**	research and development
LA	Los Angeles		**PDA**	personal digital assistant
CEO	chief executive officer		**VAT**	value added tax

First Syllable of a Word

re	regarding		**pop**	population
esp	especially		**exp**	experiment
min	minimum		**Wed**	Wednesday
max	maximum		**Aug**	August

First Syllable, Plus an Additional Letter or Syllable

dept	department		**info**	information
govt	government		**intro**	introduction
appt	appointment		**approx**	approximately

Omitted Vowels

hr	hour		**pls**	please
wk	week		**pd**	paid
yr	year		**pg**	page

Abbreviations for Weights and Measurements

g	gram		**oz**	ounce
kg	kilogram		**lb**	pound
l	liter		**qt**	quart
C	Celsius		**F**	Fahrenheit

> **Note**
> You can also make up your own abbreviations. Just be sure that if you make up an abbreviation, you remember what it stands for!

☑ **Check Yourself**

Work with a partner. Can you guess what word each abbreviation stands for? Find each word in the puzzle and circle it.

abbrev

adj

assoc

econ

ex

gen

lang

Mr

NW

NYC

obj

orig

poss

reg

A	S	S	O	C	I	A	T	I	O	N	A
D	A	B	B	T	O	D	E	G	R	P	B
J	C	E	J	M	P	J	Y	H	I	O	B
E	L	R	E	G	U	L	A	R	G	S	R
C	A	F	C	E	X	E	R	C	I	S	E
T	N	G	T	N	Q	X	Z	I	N	I	V
I	G	E	N	E	R	A	L	J	A	X	I
V	U	C	I	C	S	Y	A	K	L	P	A
E	A	D	N	O	R	T	H	W	E	S	T
I	G	M	J	N	T	V	B	M	L	Q	I
N	E	W	Y	O	R	K	C	I	T	Y	O
H	D	L	K	M	U	W	D	S	M	R	N
P	O	S	S	I	B	L	Y	T	N	S	U
J	A	S	S	C	I	L	E	E	O	T	V
G	K	H	L	S	F	X	F	R	E	G	O

PRACTICE

■ **EXERCISE 1**

🎧 *Listen. Write an abbreviation for each word or phrase. Use standard abbreviations or make up your own.*

1. _____   7. _____

2. _____   8. _____

3. _____   9. _____

4. _____   10. _____

5. _____   11. _____

6. _____   12. _____

■ EXERCISE 2

Use the examples of abbreviations to write shorter forms for these sentences.

1. I work approximately forty hours per week.

   I work approx 40 hrs / wk.

2. Please cancel the appointment on Wednesday, August 7.

   _____

3. The information was especially important because it was from the government.

   _____

4. The chief executive officer has the results of the research and development department experiment.

   _____

5. Last year, the population grew in several large cities, for example, New York and Los Angeles.

   _____

LISTENING TASK

In this Listening Task, you will hear a talk about four U.S. food festivals: the Yuma Lettuce Days Festival, the Little River Blue Crab Festival, the Hope Watermelon Festival, and the Gilroy Garlic Festival.

Before You Listen

A. Topic Preview *Work in groups. Discuss these questions.*

- Is there a famous food from your hometown or region? What is it? Describe it.
- Have you ever been to a food festival? Where was it? What was it like? If you have never been to a food festival, what do you imagine you could see or do there?

B. Vocabulary Preview *Match the words to their definitions. Use a dictionary if necessary. Then use the words to complete the sentences below.*

_d_ 1. festival   a. a list of instructions for cooking

___ 2. attend   b. something that someone wants to achieve

___ 3. recipe   c. to make people more aware of

___ 4. contest   d. a day or period of celebration

___ 5. promote   e. a competition to finish something first

___ 6. talent   f. a group of people who live in the same area

___ 7. race   g. to find out how heavy something is

___ 8. weigh   h. to go to an event

___ 9. goal   i. the natural ability to do something well

___ 10. community   j. a competition for a prize

11. How much does that _____? It must be 100 kilograms!

12. Why is this cake so salty? Did you follow the _____?

13. Are you planning to _____ his graduation ceremony?

14. She ran in a 10-kilometer _____ last weekend, and she won!

15. What's your _____? What do you want to do in the future?

16. I live in a very nice _____. Everyone is friendly and respectful.

17. I'm going to enter a _____ _____. I'm going to sing and dance.

18. That food _____ was amazing. It's great that the farmers could _____ their products.

C. 🎧 *Listen to the introduction to a talk about food festivals in the United States. Complete the notes with standard abbreviations or make up your own.*

food festivals - held once a _____

promote _____, bring _____ together

_____, not _____ held in summer/fall

many festivals in _____: Taste of Chicago

today: 4 _____ festivals

get _____ online - many towns promote on _____

D. Predict *Check your notes with your teacher. What other information do you think will be included in the talk?*

While You Listen

First Listening

A. 🎧 **Guided Practice** *Listen to the first half of the talk and complete the notes using abbreviations.*

<u>Yuma Lett. Dys. Fest.</u>

Yuma, AZ. - in _____ part of
_____

   - warm weather, farmers grow
     _____ during _____
   (lettuce most _____)
   _____ 50,000 attend, held in
   _____ every _____
   - started in _____
   - 3 _____
   - can see lettuce house, bus tours,
     music, dance
   recipe contest, _____ salad
   bar in _____

<u>Hope Watrmln Fest.</u>

Hope, AK. - famous: birthplace of
_____ Bill Clinton, _____
watrmlns
   - 2006: 121 _____ (world record for
     _____ watrmln)
Town had _____ fest. in 1977
   - held 4 _____ in _____
   - _____ 50,000 attend
   - Activities: music, talent show, games,
     sports (5 _____ race, eating
     _____, who can throw farthest

B. 🎧 **On Your Own** *Listen to the second half of the talk and take notes. Remember to omit any unnecessary words and use abbreviations where possible.*

Little River Blue Crab Festival -
Little River, SC

Gilroy Garlic Festival -
Gilroy, CA

C. *Work with a partner. Compare your notes from Exercises A and B.*

Second Listening

🎧 **Check Your Notes** *Listen and check your notes from First Listening. Add any information you missed or change any incorrect information. Then check your answers with your teacher.*

After You Listen

A. *Work with a partner. Look back at your notes and complete this chart.*

Events	Lettuce Days Festival	Watermelon Festival	Blue Crab Festival	Garlic Festival
Year Started				
Month Held				
Length				
Number of People				
Town, State				

B. *Work with your partner. Look at your chart from Exercise A. How are the festivals similar? Which ones would you like to attend? Why?*

C. *Work in small groups. Plan an interesting food festival for your town or city. Think about these questions. Then share your ideas with the class.*

1. What types of foods should be included?
2. When is the best time of year to have the festival? Why?
3. How long should the festival be? Where is a good place to have it?
4. What events will make the festival special?

Using Symbols

Unit Warm Up

Look at the to-do list. Do you know what the symbols mean? Compare your ideas with a partner.

To Do:

1. Call Joe at new #
2. Pick up Lisa @ 3:00
3. Get $ from ATM
4. Buy sodas & snacks
5. Stop by party ~ 8:00
6. * Call Dr. Perez

SKILL PRESENTATION

Using symbols saves you time when taking notes. Like abbreviations, you don't have to write out the complete word. You only have to write a simple symbol. Some symbols come from mathematics, but there are many others.

Study the following symbols:

#	number	←	comes from; is the result of
%	percent	↑	increases; goes up; more
$	dollar; money	↓	decreases; goes down; less
°	degree	→	leads to; produces; causes; makes

=	is; means; equal to; same as	♀	woman; women; female
≠	isn't doesn't mean; not the same as	♂	man; men; male
>	greater than; larger than; more than	∴	therefore
<	less than; smaller than, fewer than	*	important
~	about; approximately	@	at
+ *or* &	and; plus; also; more, in addition	" "	repeated words
/	per		

☑ Check Yourself

Match each symbol with its meaning.

__*g*__ 1. ♀   a. and

____ 2. ♂   b. therefore

____ 3. %   c. man; men; male

____ 4. &   d. less than; smaller than; fewer than

____ 5. ≠   e. about; approximately

____ 6. <   f. number

____ 7. ↑   g. woman; women; female

____ 8. ∴   h. isn't; doesn't mean; not the same as

____ 9. #   i. increases; goes up; more

____ 10. ~   j. percent

PRACTICE

■ EXERCISE 1

🎧 *Listen and write a symbol for each word or phrase.*

1. ____	5. ____	9. ____
2. ____	6. ____	10. ____
3. ____	7. ____	11. ____
4. ____	8. ____	12. ____

A. Work with a partner. These are some common sayings in English, written with symbols. Write the full sayings.

1. Practice → perfect.   _____Practice makes perfect._____.

2. $ talks.   _____.

3. The ↑ you have the ↑ you want.   _____.

4. Every ♂ has his price.   _____.

5. Haste → waste.   _____.

6. Time = money.   _____.

7. Oil + water don't mix.   _____.

8. There's safety in #s.   _____.

9. All roads → Rome.   _____.

10. Behind every successful ♂ is a ♀.   _____.

B. 🎧 **Listen and check your answers.**

LISTENING TASK

In this Listening Task, you will hear a talk about how men and women shop differently.

Before You Listen

A. Topic Preview Work in groups. Discuss these questions.

1. Do you enjoy shopping?

2. Where do you like to shop? Who do you usually shop with?

3. What's the last thing you bought? Why did you buy it?

4. What's the last thing you thought about buying but didn't? Why didn't you buy it?

B. Vocabulary Preview Match the words to their definitions. Use a dictionary if necessary. Then use the words to complete the sentences below.

_h_ 1. wander	a. an idea of what a particular type of person is like
____ 2. eventually	b. available to be sold
____ 3. stereotype	c. an important job that someone must do
____ 4. focus	d. a person or company that sells goods to the public

_____ 5. mission   e. give all your attention to a particular thing

_____ 6. in stock   f. talk with and show interest in something

_____ 7. engage   g. think that something is probably true

_____ 8. retailer   h. walk around an area, usually with no direction

_____ 9. back up   i. give support to

_____ 10. suspect   j. after a long time

11. These reports _____ my claim that the company is spending too much money.

12. I have my B.A. degree, but I hope to get an M.A. _____.

13. We kept Rachel's surprise party a secret. She didn't _____ a thing.

14. Not every vegetarian is thin and healthy. I think that's a _____.

15. My father is a clothing _____. His store hasn't done well this year.

16. I like salespeople who _____ me when I shop.

17. I can't study with the TV on. It's too hard to _____.

18. I finally chose the computer I wanted, but then the store didn't have it _____.

19. Please don't _____ away. Stay close so I know where you are.

20. Madeline is on a _____ to find the perfect wedding dress.

C. 🎧 *Listen to the introduction to a talk about how men and women shop differently. Use symbols to complete the notes.*

> Shopper _____ 1, walks into dept. store, wanders slowly, looks
> _____ diff items, evntully makes purch.
>
> Shopper 2, same store, goes drctly. to item, takes to cashier, puts
> _____ on counter
>
> Which shopper prbly a _____?   Which prbly a _____?

D. **Predict** *Check your notes with your teacher. What other information do you think will be included in the talk?*

While You Listen

First Listening

A. 🎧 **Guided Practice** *Listen to the first half of the talk and use symbols to complete the notes.*

Shopper _____ 1: _____ likely to be _____

" # 2: " " to be _____

Accord to study called: "_____ Buy, _____ Shop,"

- Amer. _____ focus _____ on shopping expernce _____ persnl attention

- _____ focus: get job done

- ♂ _____ _____ also react diff. to salesppl

- Most imp to ♂: want help finding item qckly, then help _____ checking out

_____ imp to _____: salesppl familiar w/ products, can help them decide

best item (this _____ store loyalty)

Attitudes to salesppl reflect diffs btwn _____

What _____ ♀ & ♂ so angry never return?

for _____, salesppl act rudely, ignore

" _____, lazy salesppl, _____ won't check stock , don't take them
to item

_____ _____ more personal - want salesppl who engage them

_____ want to be engaged too, but _____ imp than getting item

_____ getting out qckly

B. 🎧 **On Your Own** *Listen to the second half of the talk and take notes on a separate piece of paper. Remember to use symbols and abbreviations and omit any unnecessary words.*

C. *Work with a partner. Compare your notes from Exercises A and B.*

🎧 **Check Your Notes** *Listen and check your notes from First Listening. Add any information you missed or change any incorrect information. Then check your answers with your teacher.*

After You Listen

■ EXERCISE 1

A. *Work with a partner. Look back at your notes. Then read the descriptions in the chart. Do they describe women, men, or both women and men? Check (✓) your answers. Then compare your chart with a partner.*

According to the study, this group …	♀	♂	♀&♂
1. walks directly to an item they want when shopping			
2. looks at different items in a store			
3. focuses more on the shopping experience			
4. wants salespeople who are familiar with store items			
5. wants help at the checkout counter			
6. wants to engage with salespeople			
7. reports problems while shopping			
8. feels that not enough parking at a store is a big problem			
9. goes into a store to buy something			
10. is traditionally seen as a hunter			

B. *Work with a partner. Discuss these questions.*

1. Which descriptions in Exercise A are true for you? Which are true for people you know?

2. What's important to you when you shop? What's not important?

3. What do you think your biggest "problem" is when you shop?

4. What do you think would be difficult about being a salesperson?

5. Which store in your city or town offers good customer service? What makes the service good?

■ **EXERCISE 2**

A. *Work with a partner. Do you think you're a shopaholic (someone who shops too much)? Fill in the bubbles to take this quiz and find out.*

Are you a shopaholic?

1. What do you like to do in your free time?
   - ⓐ hang out with friends
   - ⓑ window shop
   - ⓒ buy new clothes or electronics

2. How many times a month do you go shopping?
   - ⓐ 0-2
   - ⓑ 3-6
   - ⓒ more than 7

3. What do you do when you walk into a store?
   - ⓐ get what I need and leave quickly
   - ⓑ walk around and just look at things
   - ⓒ buy something, even if I don't need it

4. What do you do when you see a sale sign in a window?
   - ⓐ keep walking
   - ⓑ go inside and see if I need anything
   - ⓒ walk in as quickly as possible

5. Are there price tags still on any clothing items in your closet?
   - ⓐ No.
   - ⓑ Yes, because I'm planning to return something.
   - ⓒ Yes. I remove the tags when I decide to wear the clothing.

6. If you get $50 for your birthday, what would you do?
   - ⓐ save it all
   - ⓑ save some and spend some
   - ⓒ spend it all

7. How would you feel if you came back from a store without any purchases?
   - ⓐ Great – I didn't spend any money.
   - ⓑ OK, but I might spend the money somewhere else.
   - ⓒ I'd feel like I failed.

8. Your friends invite you to go shopping, but you don't have any money. Would you go?

(a.) No way.

(b.) Yes, but I'd leave my credits cards at home.

(c.) Yes, and I'd take my credit cards.

9. Do you know the names of the salespeople in your favorite stores?

(a.) No.

(b.) No, but they recognize me.

(c.) Of course!

10. Have you ever bought something you couldn't afford?

(a.) No, never.

(b.) Yes, but I felt terrible about it.

(c.) Yes, and I still do.

B. *Count your a, b, and c answers from the quiz. Then read the description that matches your answers. Do you think it's accurate? Why or why not?*

Mostly *a* Answers	Mostly *b* Answers	Mostly *c* Answers
You're definitely not a shopaholic. Spending money makes you nervous.	You aren't a shopaholic. You have a good balance between saving and spending.	You may be a shopaholic. Do you shop because you want to avoid other things in your life? Be careful this doesn't lead to money problems.

Determining What's Important

Unit Warm Up

Work with a partner. Read these sentences from a lecture about effective note-taking. Number the sentences in order from 1 to 8. Then compare your answers with a partner.

_____ Like abbreviations, using symbols saves you time.

_____ Third, try to use symbols when taking notes.

__1__ There are three points I want to make about effective note-taking.

_____ However, be sure you can recognize any abbreviations you make up yourself.

_____ Second, it's a good idea to use abbreviations in your notes.

_____ It's impossible to write down everything, so take short notes instead.

_____ First, don't write down everything you hear.

_____ To summarize, don't write down everything you hear. And be sure to use abbreviations and symbols.

SKILL PRESENTATION

When you take notes, you need to recognize and write down the most important information. Speakers often give clues about the most important information in a talk. For example, they may number key points, add new or opposing ideas, or repeat important information. Listening for these clues can help you organize the key points in your notes.

Numbering Key Points

One way that speakers emphasize important information is by first introducing how many key points they will discuss and then numbering those key points one by one during the talk.

There are **five things** that I will discuss ….

There are **five important points** that I want to make …

The **first / second / third point** is …

Number 1 / 2 / 3 …

Adding and Opposing Ideas

Speakers often give specific details during a talk. They may add ideas or express opposing ideas about the topic. Not every new or opposing idea is necessarily important, but it's very helpful to recognize the phrases speakers use to introduce any additional or opposing ideas.

Adding Ideas	Opposing Ideas
And it's important to know that….	**But** this isn't always true …
Another thing that's important is …	**However**, there are exceptions …
In addition, we can see that …	**On the other hand**, we know that …
I'd **also** like to mention that …	This is not always the case, **though** …

Repeating Ideas

Speakers often repeat the most important information. They may repeat a key point within the body of the talk or repeat or review the main points of the entire talk in the conclusion. Speakers often use certain phrases to signal that they are repeating key points. Listening carefully for these phrases is an excellent way to check that you understood the main ideas of the talk.

To summarize …

Once again, the most important points are …

Let me go over what we talked about …

Now **let's review** what we discussed: …

☑ Check Yourself

A. *Copy the chart on the next page on notepaper. Write the phrases below in the correct places in the chart. Then compare with a partner.*

However, there are exceptions to this …

There are five things that I will discuss …

The first / second / third point is …

Another thing that's important is …

Now let's review what we discussed …

To summarize …

I'd also like to mention that …

This is not always the case though …

And it's important to know that …

Number 1 / 2 / 3 …

But this isn't always true …

Once again, the most important points are …

Numbering Key Points	Adding Ideas	Opposing Ideas	Repeating Ideas
		However, there are exceptions to this ...	

B. 🎧 **Listen and check your answers.**

PRACTICE

■ EXERCISE 1

A. *Write the phrases in the correct order. Then compare with a partner.*

1. that / important / make / five / are / to / I / there / points / want
   There are five important points that I want to make. ...

2. will / things / discuss / are / there / five / I / that
   _____ ...

3. that's / another / is / thing / important
   _____ ...

4. to / like / also / that / mention / I'd
   _____ ...

5. hand / know / on / that / we / the / other /
   _____ ...

6. is / case / though / this / always / not / the
   _____ ...

7. we / about / go / over / me / what / let / talked
   _____ ...

8. are / important / again / most / once / the / points
   _____ ...

B. 🎧 **Listen and check your answers.**

■ EXERCISE 2

🎧 *Listen to a student give a short talk on why* Star Wars *is her favorite movie.*
Complete the notes.

> ### Remember
>
> Use abbreviations and symbols in your notes where possible.

fav movie: Star Wars, orig from _____

_____ main reasons why so _____

1. story _____, action keeps you _____ from

_____ to end

2. like _____ - some in later films didn't like, but like all in

_____ film

3. _____ fanstastic; movie made before used a lot of comps, effects still

_____

LISTENING TASK

In this Listening Task, you will hear a talk about what makes a movie a cult film.

Before You Listen

A. **Topic Preview** *Read the movie titles. Which ones do you know? Which ones don't you know?*
What do you think they are about?

Night of the Living Dead	*The Rocky Horror Picture Show*
Brazil	*Star Wars*
Plan Nine from Outer Space	*Titanic*
Office Space	*Blade Runner*
Heathers	*Crouching Tiger, Hidden Dragon*

B. Vocabulary Preview *Read the sentences. Then write each underlined word or phrase next to its definition below.*

- That movie was a <u>mainstream</u> hit. Everyone knows it.
- Skateboarders have their own <u>subculture</u>. This is expressed through their fashions and lifestyle.
- This poem is so <u>obscure</u>. Very few people have ever heard of it.
- Some people think my ideas are <u>controversial</u>. Not everyone agrees with me.
- Everyone thinks this TV show is so great, but I'm not sure what the <u>appeal</u> is.
- That actress is famous for her <u>devotion</u> to animal rights.
- The <u>release</u> of her new movie has been delayed until next year.
- This DVD was a <u>box office bomb</u>. It made very little money at the theater.
- His first novel was <u>widely acclaimed</u>. It got excellent reviews from critics.
- That director is known for his <u>low-budget</u> but very successful films.

1. _____ praised by a lot of people
2. _____ a strong feeling of love or admiration
3. _____ known only by a few people
4. _____ a new movie that is available for people to see
5. _____ a culture within a larger culture
6. _____ a movie that very few people saw in theaters
7. _____ made with very little money
8. _____ the quality that makes you like something
9. _*mainstream*___ accepted or familiar to most people
10. _____ something that causes disagreement because people have different opinions about it

C. 🎧 *Listen to the introduction to a talk about cult films. Complete the notes.*

Night of the _____ Dead, Brazil, Plan _____
from Outer Space
What have in _____?
_____ mainstream films, known as cult films
What _____ these CFs?
_____

D. Predict *Check your notes with your teacher. What other information do you think will be included in the talk?*

While You Listen

First Listening

A. 🎧 **Guided Practice** *Listen to the first half of the talk and complete the notes.*

1. CFs pop w/ _____ groups

       e.g. _____, ♂ coll students, subcuture films strange, obscure

topics not pop in mainstream _____

what → CF for one, may not be true for another

     e.g. Office Space pop w/_____

     Heather speaks to _____ but not same appeal

     w/_____

2. CFs have loyal fans, show devotion in diff ways

     e.g. most famous CF: The Rocky Horror Picture Show became pop when

     theaters _____

     fans began _____

shown in theaters ever since

other ways: _____, chat room, websites

loyal fans ≠ CF

     e.g. Star Wars & Titanic lots of fans but _____

     - too _____

B. 🎧 **On Your Own** *Listen to the second half of the talk and take notes on a separate piece of paper. Remember to listen for phrases that tell you what's important.*

C. *Work with a partner. Compare your notes from Exercises A and B.*

🎧 **Check Your Notes** *Listen and check your notes from First Listening. Add any information you missed or change any incorrect information. Then check your answers with your teacher.*

After You Listen

■ **EXERCISE 1**

A. *Work with a partner. These films are all mentioned in the talk. Look back at your notes. Check (✓) the films that are cult films.*

☐ *Night of the Living Dead*   ☐ *The Rocky Horror Picture Show*

☐ *Brazil*   ☐ *Star Wars*

☐ *Plan Nine from Outer Space*   ☐ *Titanic*

☐ *Office Space*   ☐ *Blade Runner*

☐ *Heathers*   ☐ *Crouching Tigers, Hidden Dragon*

B. *Read each statement. Write **T** for true or **F** for false. Then correct the false statements.*

__T__ **1.** Cult films are only popular with certain groups of people.

_____ **2.** Cult films can be strange or obscure.

_____ **3.** Cult films are always controversial.

_____ **4.** *Heathers* is a very popular cult film among older viewers.

_____ **5.** Cult films have loyal fans.

_____ **6.** The most famous cult film of all time is *Office Space*.

_____ **7.** The audience participates when viewing *The Rocky Horror Picture Show*.

_____ **8.** All mainstream films with loyal fans are cult films.

_____ **9.** Many cult films don't make much money.

_____ **10.** The speaker says that some cult films are "so bad they're good."

_____ **11.** Some people believe that *Night of the Living Dead* is "the worst movie ever made."

_____ **12.** Movies seldom become cult films as soon as they appear.

■ EXERCISE 2

A. Work with a partner. Read these descriptions of other films. Do you think they are cult films? Why or why not? Discuss your reasons.

1. *The Big Lebowski* (1998) didn't do well on its release but received favorable reviews. Popular at midnight screenings, fans often quote lines from the movie. There are even "Lebowski Fests" in some U.S. cities, with games, contests, and fans in costumes.

2. *The Adventures of Pluto Nash* (2002) was a huge box-office bomb. It made only $7 million in theaters and, adding together production and marketing, cost $120 million to make. It received terrible reviews and seems to have very few fans, even on video.

3. *Robot Monster* (1953) has bad writing and terrible acting but has become a favorite of science fiction fans. It was made over four days for just $16,000. The budget didn't allow for a robot suit so the director's friend acted in a gorilla suit and helmet.

4. *Shrek 2* made more than $100 million in its opening weekend and remained in the top 10 for ten weeks. A hit with critics and fans of all ages, it was the most successful film of 2004 and went on to make nearly $1 billion worldwide.

5. *The Blair Witch Project* (1999) received positive reviews on its release. It was a huge mainstream success, making more than $250 million worldwide. It cost very little to make and is considered the first movie that was marketed on the Internet.

6. *This is Spinal Tap* (1984) had mixed reviews on its release but was somewhat successful. The film developed a huge following when it was released on video. The film has continued to attract new fans with each new video version that is released.

B. Work with a partner. Discuss these questions.

1. Which of the cult films in this unit have you heard of?

2. Have you seen any of the films discussed in this unit? What did you think of them?

3. What other cult films do you know? Have you seen them? How would you describe them?

4. Have you seen any films that are "so bad they're good"? What did you like about them?

5. Are there any recent movies that you think could become cult films someday? Why?

Evaluating Your Notes

In this unit, you will have a chance to review and evaluate the note-taking skills you learned in Units 1 through 4. You will also think about ways to improve your note-taking.

Remember

These are the most important skills for taking notes:

1. **Omit unnecessary words** Don't include function words, such as articles (*a, an, the*), prepositions (*in, to, with, for*), and the verb *to be* (*is, are, were*).
2. **Use abbreviations** You can use standard abbreviations (*U.S.* for *United States*, *km* for *kilometer*, *w/* for *with*). You can also use the first few letters of words (e.g., *prelim* for *preliminary*) or omit letters—usually vowels—from the middle of words (e.g., *intl* for *international*).
3. **Use symbols** For example, you can use the symbol → to mean *causes* or *becomes* or the symbol + to mean *and*, *also*, or *in addition to*.
4. **Write only important points and ideas** Don't take notes on unimportant details or examples.
5. **Listen for phrases that tell you what's important** These phrases tell you if the speaker is listing important points, adding opposing points, or repeating ideas.

Unit Warm Up

In this unit, you will listen to a business lecture about the "life cycle" of a product.

Work in groups. Look at the graph and discuss the questions.

The life cycle of a product

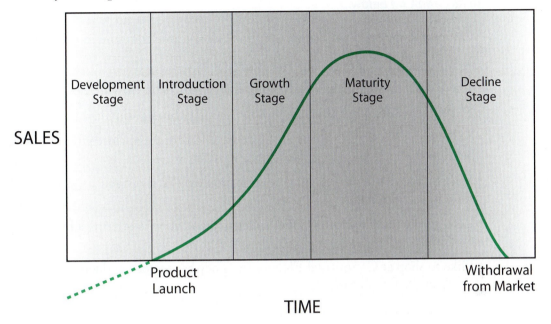

1. What does "life cycle" means when talking about living things? What do you think it means when talking about a product?

2. Read the titles of the stages. Look up any words you don't know.

3. What do you think happens to a product in each stage? Write the name of the stage next to each action.

   Stage

   _____ The company starts to sell the product.

   _____ The company stops selling the product.

   _____ People begin to learn about the product; sales go up.

   _____ Sales start to go down; the company offers lower prices.

   _____ The company tests the new product.

4. Can you think of examples of products you know that are in each of the stages?

Before You Listen

A. Vocabulary Preview *Read the sentences. Then write each underlined word next to its definition below.*

- Online shopping is a modern <u>concept</u>. It only became common in the 1990s.
- Every living <u>organism</u> needs a way to get energy.
- These days, most companies <u>advertise</u> their products on the Internet.
- The museum is open to the <u>public</u> from Tuesday through Sunday.
- There are so many restaurants in this town. Many of them close after a short time because there is too much <u>competition</u>.
- You don't have to spend an hour on that problem. I'll show you a <u>shortcut</u>, and you can solve it in ten minutes.
- Let's go shopping tomorrow. Shay's Department Store is offering a big <u>discount</u> on all clothing.
- I like to shop at Continental Electronics. They have good products and provide good service for <u>consumers</u>.

1. _____ a lower price
2. _____ a quicker, more direct way to do something
3. _____ a thought or idea
4. _____ a situation when many businesses try to sell the same thing
5. _____ everyone; all the people in an area
6. _____ something that is alive
7. _____ people who buy things from a store or company
8. _____ try to get people to buy a product using the Internet or TV

B. 🎧 *Listen to the introduction to a lecture about the life cycle of a product. The speaker wrote notes on the board. Complete the speaker's notes.*

> Today's lecture: _____ stages of product life cycle
>
> From _____ = devlopmt stage, until decline stage, when company _____ selling it
>
> Product = living _____
>
> Comp. introduces new product (Product is _____)
>
> Product devlps and _____
>
> Product reaches maturity stage = person or an animal becomes _____
>
> When product no longer useful or _____ (dies)

C. Predict *Work with a partner. Compare your notes from Exercise B. What information do you think the speaker will include in the lecture? What questions do you have about product life cycle?*

While You Listen

In this section, you will listen to the lecture about product life cycle. The lecture is divided into four parts. After each part, you will hear and answer some questions to help you evaluate your note-taking skills.

Evaluation Practice 1

A. 🎧 *Listen to the first part of the lecture and take notes on a separate piece of paper. Remember to omit unnecessary words and use abbreviations and symbols where possible.*

B. 🎧 *Look at your notes from Exercise A. Listen to the evaluation questions and write short answers. Then compare your answers with a partner.*

1. Stage _____

2. Speaker's opinion _____

3. What the company does _____

4. Ways they advertise: _____

5. **Did you ...**

	Yes	No
• omit unnecessary words?	☐	☐
• use abbreviations where possible?	☐	☐
• use symbols?	☐	☐

Evaluation Practice 2

A. 🎧 *Listen to the next part of the lecture and continue your notes.*

B. 🎧 *Look at your notes from Exercise A. Listen to the evaluation questions and write short answers. Then compare your answers with a partner.*

1. Second stage _____

2. What happens _____

3. Next stage _____

4. What happens _____

5. **Did you note...**

	Yes	No
• the important point the speaker makes about the introductory stage?	☐	☐
• the opposing idea the speaker gives about the growth stage?	☐	☐

Evaluation Practice 3

A. 🎧 *Listen to the next part of the lecture and continue your notes.*

B. 🎧 *Look at your notes from Exercise A. Listen to the evaluation questions and write short answers. Then compare your answers with a partner.*

1. Fourth stage _____

2. What happens _____

3. **Did you note ...**

	Yes	No
• the reasons prices come down in this stage?	☐	☐
• examples of ways companies try to keep their business ?	☐	☐

Evaluation Practice 4

A. 🎧 *Listen to the last part of the lecture and continue your notes.*

B. 🎧 *Look at your notes from Exercise A. Listen to the evaluation questions and write short answers. Then compare your answers with a partner.*

1. Final stage _____

2. What happens _____

3. Reasons _____

4. **Did you note …**

	Yes	No
• the examples of products in this stage?	☐	☐
• the key point about the life cycle description?	☐	☐

Final Self-Evaluation

A. *Think about your note-taking skills. In which areas do you feel confident? Which areas still need improvement? Check (✓) the columns to complete the self-evaluation.*

Unit 1 – Omitting Unnecessary Words

	Excellent	Good	Needs Improvement
Writing down important content words			
Omitting function words			

Unit 2 – Using Abbreviations

	Excellent	Good	Needs Improvement
Using standard abbreviations			
Making up your own abbreviations			
Understanding abbreviations in your notes			

Unit 3 – Using Symbols

	Excellent	Good	Needs Improvement
Using symbols where possible			
Understanding symbols in your notes			

Unit 4 – Determining What's Important

	Excellent	Good	Needs Improvement
Understanding the main topic			
Writing only important words and ideas			
Listening for phrases that tell when the speaker adds a new idea			
Listening for phrases that tell when the speaker offers an opposing idea			
Listening for repeated information			

B. *Did you mark any areas that need improvement? If so, go back and review the Skill Presentation sections in Units 1 through 4.*

After You Listen

A. *Work with a partner. Compare your notes from the lecture. Are they the similar? Discuss any differences. Add any information you missed and correct any incorrect information.*

B. *Work with your partner. Use your notes to answer the questions about the lecture.*

1. Which statement best summarizes the whole lecture?

   a. The speaker disagrees with the concept of product life cycle.

   b. The speaker compares the life of a product to the life of a living organism.

   c. The speaker gives examples of products in all of the stages.

   d. The speaker talks about how companies develop products.

2. The development stage includes work done on a product _____.

   a. after the company begins to sell it

   b. before the company begins to sell it

   c. when sales slow down

3. According to the speaker, companies usually test the product during the _____.

   a. introductory stage

   b. development stage

   c. decline stage

4. The speaker believes that the _____ stage is the most important.

   a. development

   b. introductory

   c. growth

   d. maturity

5. During the growth stage, _____ are high.

    a. sales and competition

    b. prices and competition

    c. prices and sales

6. According to the speaker many new products _____.

    a. never enter the growth stage

    b. stay in the decline stage for a long time

    c. enter the development stage early

7. During the maturity stage, the company _____.

    a. slows down

    b. makes products faster

    c. stops selling the product

8. During the maturity stage, companies often _____.

    a. keep prices the same

    b. raise prices

    c. lower their prices

9. A change in fashion can cause _____.

    a. a product to decline

    b. prices to decrease

    c. an increase in competition

10. Which of these opinions would the speaker probably agree with?

    a. Most products do not follow the product life cycle, so it is not a useful concept.

    b. Every product follows the product life cycle, but some products take more time.

    c. The product life cycle is a useful model, even though it is not true about every product.

C. **Did taking notes help you answer the questions about the lecture? In what way? Share your ideas with the class.**

Note-Taking Practice

In this unit, you will practice listening to a longer lecture and taking notes. This is your chance to practice all of the skills you have learned in Part 3.

Before you begin this unit, go back to the Self-Evaluation in Unit 5 on pages 133–134. Think about the areas you feel still need improvement and try to focus on those skills as you listen and take notes in this unit.

Unit Warm Up

You will listen to a talk about the common cold.

Work in groups. Discuss these questions.

- How often do you catch a cold?

- What are some common ways people treat colds in your country?

- How do you usually treat yourself when you have a cold?

- Do you think scientists will ever find a way to stop people from getting the common cold? Why or why not?

Before You Listen

A. Vocabulary Preview *Read the sentences. Then write each underlined word next to its definition below.*

- If you get a cut, you should clean it carefully, or you might get an <u>infection</u>.
- Sam gets sick often. He missed five days of work last month because of <u>illness</u>.
- José was lucky. He only had a <u>mild</u> form of the flu, not a bad one.
- A headache is often one of the first <u>symptoms</u> of a cold.
- Are you OK? That sounds like a bad <u>cough</u>. Would you like a drink of water?
- Mei Li hasn't eaten anything for days. She has a bad stomach <u>virus</u>.
- Do you think scientists will ever find a <u>cure</u> for the common cold?
- If you feel very warm, you may have a <u>fever</u>. Check your temperature and get into bed right away.
- A hot bath and pain medicine are common <u>treatments</u> for sore, tired muscles.
- This is a very serious <u>disease</u>. Many people die from it each year.

1. _____ something that makes a sickness go away completely
2. _____ ways of making a sick person feel better
3. _____ a sickness caused by tiny living things entering the body
4. _____ body temperature that is above normal
5. _____ a very small living thing that causes you to get sick
6. _____ not causing much discomfort; not very strong
7. _____ the signs of a sickness
8. _____ a sickness
9. _____ stop something from happening
10. _____ air and sound that suddenly comes from the throat, often when you are sick

B. **Predict** *What do you know about the common cold? Work in pairs. Check (✓) True or False for each statement. Then compare answers with another pair.*

		True	False
1.	No one really knows what causes the common cold.	☐	☐
2.	We can only get colds from other people who have a cold.	☐	☐
3.	It is easier to get a cold if you are cold or wet.	☐	☐
4.	The best way to prevent colds is by washing your hands.	☐	☐
5.	Older people have more colds than children.	☐	☐
6.	Scientists are close to finding a cure for the common cold.	☐	☐
7.	You should eat chicken soup if you have a cold.	☐	☐
8.	Influenza (flu) is a more serious illness than the common cold.	☐	☐

While You Listen

First Listening

A. 🎧 **On Your Own** *Listen to the first part of the lecture on the common cold. Take notes on a separate piece of paper.*

> **Remember**
>
> 1. Omit unnecessary words
> 2. Use abbreviations and symbols where possible
> 3. Write only important points and ideas
> 4. Listen for phrases that tell you which information is important.

B. *Work with a partner. Compare your notes from Exercise A and discuss any differences.*

C. *Discuss these statements from **Before You Listen** with your partner. Use your notes from Exercise A to check your answers.*

		True	False
1.	No one really knows what causes the common cold.	☐	☐
2.	We can only get colds from other people who have a cold.	☐	☐
3.	It is easier to get a cold if you are cold or wet.	☐	☐
4.	The best way to prevent colds is by washing your hands.	☐	☐

D. 🎧 **On Your Own** *Listen to the next part of the lecture on the common cold. Continue taking your notes.*

E. *Work with a partner. Compare your notes from Exercise D and discuss any differences.*

F. *Discuss these statements from Before You Listen with your partner. Use your notes from Exercise D to check your answers.*

	True	False
1. Older people have more colds than children.	☐	☐
2. Scientists are close to finding a cure for the common cold.	☐	☐
3. You should each chicken soup if you have a cold.	☐	☐
4. Influenza (flu) is a more serious illness than the common cold.	☐	☐

Second Listening

🎧 **Check Your Notes** *Listen and check your notes from First Listening. Add any information you missed or change any incorrect information. Then check your answers with your teacher.)*

After You Listen

A. *Work with a partner. Use your notes to answer the questions about the lecture. Circle the best answer.*

1. The speaker's main purpose is to _____.

   a. discuss how scientists will find a cure for the common cold

   b. talk about how colds and the flu are the same and different

   c. give listeners some basic information about common colds

2. We can infer that colds are called "common colds" because _____.

   a. they are difficult to cure

   b. many people get them

   c. they have a lot in common with the flu

3. According to the speaker, most mild colds last _____.

   a. two or three days

   b. three or four days

   c. several weeks

4. Scientists learned what causes colds _____.

   a. in 1946

   b. in 1964

   c. in 1994

5. There are about _____ viruses that cause colds.

   a. 12

   b. 20

   c. 200

(continued)

6. To prevent colds, the speaker recommends _____.

   a. washing hands often

   b. wearing warm clothing

   c. staying indoors in winter

7. According to the speaker, why are colds more common during the winter?

   a. The air is dryer.

   b. People spend more time inside.

   c. Cold viruses grow stronger in colder weather.

8. The speaker says that in warmer places, colds are more common during _____.

   a. the dry season

   b. the winter months

   c. the rainy season

9. Which of these groups gets colds more often?

   a. baby boys

   b. teenagers

   c. baby girls

10. Which of these statements would the author probably agree with?

    a. Cold medicines can help people feel better when they have a cold.

    b. There are no helpful treatments for the common cold.

    c. People should not use medicine to treat the symptoms of colds.

11. According to the speaker, what is the reason a cure for the cold may never be found?

    a. There are too many symptoms.

    b. Most treatments aren't useful.

    c. There are too many cold viruses.

12. Check (✓) the correct column(s).

A Cold	The Flu	
		can cause a cough
		usually causes a fever
		makes people feel weak
		does not last as long
		can be dangerous

B. **Compare your answers with a partner. Then check your answers with your teacher.**

C. **Exchange notes with your partner. Take turns using each other's notes to give a summary of the lecture. Tell your partner any places where you can't understand the notes.**

Listening
for Pleasure

A TV Game Show

Unit Warm Up

In this unit, you will listen to a TV game show about people with unusual jobs.

Work with a partner. Look at the unusual jobs below. Discuss these questions.

- Which job do you think is the easiest? Which job is the most difficult? Why?

- What would you like about each job? What wouldn't you like?

- Name another unusual job. Do you think you'd be good at it? Why or why not?

stand-up comedian

bull rider

ice artist

Introduction

Do you ever watch TV game shows in your own language? Do you ever watch them in English? These kinds of shows can be a fun way to build your skills at listening to forms of English, especially questions and answers. Of course, you can learn lots of other interesting information from game shows, too!

Ann Brown is a contestant on the TV game show "What's My Job?" The show features people with unusual jobs. Ann can ask ten *yes/no* questions to try and guess a person's job. Play the game along with Ann

LISTENING TASK

Round 1

Useful Terms

industry business activity

emergency an unexpected or dangerous situation

skyscraper a very tall building in a city

miserable very unhappy

A. 🎧 *Listen to Ann ask Mike these ten questions about his job. Take notes on his answers. Then guess the job.*

Questions	Notes
1. Are you in the entertainment business?	
2. Do you work in the food industry?	
3. Do you work in an office?	
4. Do you work outside?	
5. Would someone call you if there was an emergency?	
6. Do you repair or build things?	
7. Do you clean something?	
8. Is your job dangerous?	
9. Do you work high above the ground?	
10. Do you work on the outside of skyscrapers?	

My guess: _____

B. 🎧 *Listen to Ann guess the job. Did she guess correctly? Did you guess correctly?*

C. 🎧 *Listen to what Mike says he likes and dislikes about his job.*

D. *Work with a partner. What would you like about Mike's job? What wouldn't you like? Why?*

Round 2

Useful Terms

factory a building where goods or products are made

laboratory a room in which scientists do tests

consistent having the same quality

blend a mixture of two or more things

A. 🎧 *Listen to Ann ask Wendy these ten questions about her job. Take notes on her answers. Then guess the job.*

Questions	Notes
1. Do you work inside?	
2. Are you in the entertainment business?	
3. Are you in the food industry?	
4. Does your job require you to cook?	
5. Do you work in a factory?	
6. Do you work in a laboratory?	
7. Do you taste or test something?	
8. Is it something we eat every day?	
9. Do you taste something that is hot?	
10. Is this something people often drink in the morning?	

My guess: _____

B. 🎧 *Listen to Ann guess the job. Did she guess correctly? Did you guess correctly?*

C. 🎧 *Listen to what Wendy says she likes and dislikes about her job.*

D. *Work with a partner. What would you like about Wendy's job? What wouldn't you like? Why?*

Round 3

Useful Terms

uniform clothes worn to identify someone's job

ideal the best that something could be

frustrated annoyed because you can't do what you want

animation TV show or movies that use drawings that appear to move

A. 🎧 *Listen to Ann ask Josh these ten questions about his job. Take notes on his answers. Then guess the job.*

Questions	Notes
1. Does your job require you to wear a uniform?	
2. Are you in the entertainment business?	
3. Are you ever on TV?	
4. Do you perform in front of people?	
5. Do you create something?	
6. Does your job involve computers?	
7. Is drawing part of your job?	
8. Do you draw things that appear in a book?	
9. Is it something that young people like?	
10. Are your drawings things that people like to collect?	

My guess: _____

B. 🎧 *Listen to Ann guess the job. Did she guess correctly? Did you guess correctly?*

C. 🎧 *Listen to what Josh says he likes and dislikes about his job.*

D. *Work with a partner. What would you like about Josh's job? What wouldn't you like? Why?*

After You Listen

A. *Work in a group. Read about these "hot jobs of the future." Then discuss the questions.*

Distance Educator Develops new techniques for better online learning	**Space Tour Guide** Acts as a tour guide for tourists in space	**Avatar Security Advisor** Designs, creates, and protects the virtual you
Health Advisor Helps people meet their diet and exercise goals	**Simplicity Engineer** Suggests ways to make technology and processes in a company easier	**Robot Mechanic** Repairs robots to help keep them running smoothly
Organic Food Producer Improves farming techniques without the use of chemicals	**Cloud Controller** Fights climate change by helping clouds reflect sunlight better	**Local Expert** Offers local products and services to better compete against large companies

1. Which of these jobs would interest you the most? Why?
2. What other jobs do you think will be needed in the future?
3. What jobs do you think will no longer exist in the future? Why?
4. What would be your ideal job?

B. *Choose one of the jobs in Exercise A or make up an interesting job of your own. Imagine you have this job. Take notes on what your job is like.*

Job:		
What I do	**Where I work**	**Who or what I work with**
What I wear	**My job responsibilities**	**Other information**

C. *Work in groups. Take turns playing the game "What's my job?" Your group members can ask you ten Yes/No questions and then guess your job.*

Example

A: *Do you work outside?*

B: *Yes, most of the time.*

C: *Do you work with food?*

B: *No, not really.*

D: *Does your job involve driving?*

Urban Legends

Unit Warm Up

In this unit, you will listen to several short stories called "urban legends." Urban legends are a special type of story.

Work with a partner. Read the article, "What are Urban Legends." Then check (✓) True or False for each statement below.

	True	False
1. Urban legends are stories about cities.	☐	☐
2. Urban legends are usually about modern life.	☐	☐
3. Today, urban legends often get passed around on the Internet.	☐	☐
4. Urban legends are always false.	☐	☐
5. Urban legends usually have only one version.	☐	☐
6. Some urban legends are frightening or shocking.	☐	☐

Q: So, what are urban legends?

A: Well, urban means city. And legends are …

Q: Legends are stories, I know. So, urban legends are just stories about cities?

A: No, not really. You see, a lot of the legends from the past, such as fairy tales, took place in rural areas, in forests, and so on. So … these modern stories are called urban legends to contrast them with the older stories.

Q: So urban legends don't always take place in big cities?

A: No, not at all. Some do, some don't.

Q: But what are urban legends?

A: They are stories that are passed on from person to person about modern life. They are usually surprising, and sometimes they are really shocking. Sometimes they are just funny.

Q: Why do people tell these stories?

A: Well sometimes, these stories teach a lesson. They teach you to be careful. In these stories, something terrible happens, or it almost happens. If you are not careful, the

(continued)

same terrible thing can happen to you. But not all urban legends teach lessons. For as long as there have been humans, there has been storytelling. People just like to tell stories and to hear stories.

Q: How do these stories get passed around?

A: In the past, one person told another, and that person told several other people, and so on. That's true today too, but these days, a lot of stories get passed around very quickly on the Internet. Someone sends you an interesting story in an email, you send a copy of the email to your friends, and they send a copy to people they know.

Q: Are urban legends always false?

A: No. Most of them are. Sometimes people say, "Oh, that's just an urban legend" and they mean, "That's not true." But sometimes urban legends are partially true. In other words they are based on a true event, something that really happened, but the story has been changed. And sometimes, urban legends are completely true. But even when an urban legend is not true, it is always told as if it were true!

Q: What else can you tell me about urban legends?

A: Well, for one thing, there are many versions of them. Every time someone tells a story, it changes a little. And they are usually set in the places where they are told.

Q: What do you mean?

A: If you live in Boston and someone tells you an urban legend, it probably will begin, "This happened right here in Boston." If you hear that same story in Sydney, it might begin, "This happened here in Sydney." And to make it more believable, storytellers usually say that they heard it from someone who is believable, someone that they know. For example, they'll say, "I heard this story from a friend of a friend of mine …"

Q: Anything else?

A: Well … just that a lot of people enjoy hearing or reading urban legends—there are a lot of sites on the Internet about urban legends. And people enjoy hearing these stories and telling their friends. Even ones that are frightening or shocking!

Introduction

Do you enjoy reading stories? Short stories like urban legends are great for learning English. You can read books of short stories, but you can also listen to audio versions on CD or on the Internet. Listening to stories in English can help you learn the natural rhythm of English.

LISTENING TASK

Legend 1 Danger from Behind

This is a classic urban legend that has been told for many years and in many places around the world.

Useful Terms

gas station	a place to buy gasoline and sometimes snacks, drinks, and other items
flash headlights	to signal someone by turning the headlights on a car quickly on and off
highway	an important and well-traveled road
country road	a less important road in an agricultural area
prison	a building where people are held for committing crimes

🎧 *Listen to Legend 1. Then discuss these questions in small groups.*

1. Who is the woman in the story? What is she doing?

2. The woman in the story is surprised when the man calls the police. Why?

3. Were you surprised by the ending of the story? Why or why not?

4. What lesson or lessons do you think this story teaches the listener?

5. Do you believe that this story is completely true, partially true, or completely false? Why?

Legend 2 The Math Problems

A story similar to this one has been told on university campuses all over the world.

Useful Terms

oversleep	sleep too long
in a panic	afraid; stressed; nervous
get in touch with	make contact with; speak with

🎧 *Listen to Legend 2. Then discuss these questions in small groups.*

1. Why does the woman tell the man the story about George?

2. Why was George in a panic?

3. Why did George's teacher call him?

4. Do you believe that this story is completely true, partially true, or completely false? Why?

Legend 3 The Exploding Cactus

Useful Terms

cactus   a desert plant with sharp points

puzzled   confused

scorpion   a tropical insect-like animal with pinchers and a curling tail with a poisonous tip

lay eggs   to produce eggs

hatch   to come out of an egg

explode   to break open suddenly and violently; to blow up

🎧 *Listen to Legend 3. Then discuss these questions in small groups.*

1. Why did the man tell this story?

2. Why did the woman hurry out of her house?

3. Do you believe that this story is completely true, partially true, or completely false? Why?.

Legend 4 The Flying Cat

Useful Terms

fire chief the boss of a fire department

firefighters emergency workers who put out fires

🎧 *Listen to Legend 4. Then discuss these questions in small groups.*

1. Why did the fire chief decide to help the woman?

2. Why couldn't the firefighters climb the tree?

3. The storyteller says that Cupcake is "lucky." Why?

4. Do you believe that this story is completely true, partially true, or completely false? Why?

After You Listen

Work in groups. Choose one of these story titles and write an urban legend. Then share your story with the class.

Cat Rescues Family from Fire	Alligator in the Bathtub
The Never-Ending Computer Game	Lost Dog Returns after Ten Years
The Boy Who Watched Too Much TV	The Spider That Grew (and Grew)

Credits